Joseph R. Ferrari
Judith G. Chapman
Editors

Educating Students to Make-a-Difference: Community-Based Service Learning

Educating Students to Make-a-Difference: Community-Based Service Learning has been co-published simultaneously as *Journal of Prevention & Intervention in the Community*, Volume 18, Numbers 1/2 1999.

*Pre-publication
REVIEWS,
COMMENTARIES,
EVALUATIONS . . .*

"**P**resents an overview of community-based service learning among students from seventh grade to medical school. . . . This edited volume will especially appeal to those involved in community-based service learning programs."

Clifford R. O'Donnell, PhD
*Director of Community
and Culture Graduate Program
University of Hawaii*

Educating Students to Make-a-Difference: Community-Based Service Learning

Educating Students to Make-a-Difference: Community-Based Service Learning has been co-published simultaneously as *Journal of Prevention & Intervention in the Community*™, Volume 18, Numbers 1/2 1999.

The *Journal of Prevention & Intervention in the Community*™ Monographic "Separates" (formerly the Prevention in Human Services series)*

For information on previous issues of Prevention in Human Services, edited by Robert E. Hess, please contact: The Haworth Press, Inc., 10 Alice Street, Binghamton, NY 13904-1580 USA.

Below is a list of "separates," which in serials librarianship means a special issue simultaneously published as a special journal issue or double-issue *and* as a "separate" hardbound monograph. (This is a format which we also call a "DocuSerial.")

"Separates" are published because specialized libraries or professionals may wish to purchase a specific thematic issue by itself in a format which can be separately cataloged and shelved, as opposed to purchasing the journal on an on-going basis. Faculty members may also more easily consider a "separate" for classroom adoption.

"Separates" are carefully classified separately with the major book jobbers so that the journal tie-in can be noted on new book order slips to avoid duplicate purchasing.

You may wish to visit Haworth's website at . . .

http://www.haworthpressinc.com

. . . to search our online catalog for complete tables of contents of these separates and related publications.

You may also call 1-800-HAWORTH (outside US/Canada: 607-722-5857), or Fax 1-800-895-0582 (outside US/Canada: 607-771-0012), or e-mail at:

getinfo@haworthpressinc.com

Educating Students to Make-a-Difference: Community-Based Service Learning, edited by Joseph R. Ferrari, PhD, and Judith G. Chapman, PhD (Vol. 18(1/2), 1999). *"There is something here for everyone interested in the social psychology of service-learning." (Frank Bernt, PhD, Associate Professor, St. Joseph's University)*

Program Implementation in Preventive Trials, edited by Joseph A. Durlak and Joseph R. Ferrari, PhD (Vol. 17(2), 1998). *"Fills an important gap in preventive research. . . . Highlights an array of important questions related to implementation and demonstrates just how good community-based intervention programs can be when issues related to implementation are taken seriously." (Judy Primavera, PhD, Associate Professor of Psychology, Fairfield University, Fairfield, Connecticut)*

Preventing Drunk Driving, edited by Elsie R. Shore, PhD, and Joseph R. Ferrari, PhD (Vol. 17(1), 1998). *"A must read for anyone interested in reducing the needless injuries and death caused by the drunk driver." (Terrance D. Schiavone, President, National Commission Against Drunk Driving, Washington, DC)*

Manhood Development in Urban African-American Communities, edited by Roderick J. Watts, PhD, and Robert J. Jagers (Vol. 16(1/2), 1998). *"Watts and Jagers provide the much-needed foundational and baseline information and research that begins to philosophically and empirically validate the importance of understanding culture, oppression, and gender when working with males in urban African-American communities." (Paul Hill, Jr., MSW, LISW, ACSW, East End Neighborhood House, Cleveland, Ohio)*

Diversity Within the Homeless Population: Implications for Intervention, edited by Elizabeth M. Smith, PhD, and Joseph R. Ferrari, PhD (Vol. 15(2), 1997). *"Examines why homelessness is increasing, as well as treatment options, case management techniques, and community intervention programs that can be used to prevent homelessness." (American Public Welfare Association)*

Education in Community Psychology: Models for Graduate and Undergraduate Programs, edited by Clifford R. O'Donnell, PhD, and Joseph R. Ferrari, PhD (Vol. 15(1), 1997). *"An invaluable resource for students seeking graduate training in community psychology . . . [and will] also serve faculty who want to improve undergraduate teaching and graduate programs." (Marybeth Shinn, PhD, Professor of Psychology and Coordinator, Community Doctoral Program, New York University, New York, New York)*

Adolescent Health Care: Program Designs and Services, edited by John S. Wodarski, PhD, Marvin D. Feit, PhD, and Joseph R. Ferrari, PhD (Vol. 14(1/2), 1997). *Devoted to helping practitioners address the problems of our adolescents through the use of preventive interventions based on sound empirical data.*

Preventing Illness Among People with Coronary Heart Disease, edited by John D. Piette, PhD, Robert M. Kaplan, PhD, and Joseph R. Ferrari, PhD (Vol. 13(1/2), 1996). *"A useful contribution to the interaction of physical health, mental health, and the behavioral interventions for patients with CHD. " (Public Health: The Journal of the Society of Public Health)*

Sexual Assault and Abuse: Sociocultural Context of Prevention, edited by Carolyn F. Swift, PhD* (Vol. 12(2), 1995). *"Delivers a cornucopia for all who are concerned with the primary prevention of these damaging and degrading acts." (George J. McCall, PhD, Professor of Sociology and Public Administration, University of Missouri)*

International Approaches to Prevention in Mental Health and Human Services, edited by Robert E. Hess, PhD, and Wolfgang Stark* (Vol. 12(1), 1995.) *Increases knowledge of prevention strategies from around the world.*

Self-Help and Mutual Aid Groups: International and Multicultural Perspectives, edited by Francine Lavoie, PhD, Thomasina Borkman, PhD, and Benjamin Gidron* (Vol. 11(1/2), 1995). *"A helpful orientation and overview, as well as useful data and methodological suggestions." (International Journal of Group Psychotherapy)*

Prevention and School Transitions, edited by Leonard A. Jason, PhD, Karen E. Danner, and Karen S. Kurasaki, MA* (Vol. 10(2), 1994). *"A collection of studies by leading ecological and systems-oriented theorists in the area of school transitions, describing the stressors, personal resources available, and coping strategies among different groups of children and adolescents undergoing school transitions." (Reference & Research Book News)*

Religion and Prevention in Mental Health: Research, Vision, and Action, edited by Kenneth I. Pargament, PhD, Kenneth I. Maton, PhD, and Robert E. Hess, PhD* (Vol. 9(2) & 10(1), 1992). *"The authors provide an admirable framework for considering the important, yet often overlooked, differences in theological perspectives." (Family Relations)*

Families as Nurturing Systems: Support Across the Life Span, edited by Donald G. Unger, PhD, and Douglas R. Powell, PhD* (Vol. 9(1), 1991). *"A useful book for anyone thinking about alternative ways of delivering a mental health service." (British Journal of Psychiatry)*

Ethical Implications of Primary Prevention, edited by Gloria B. Levin, PhD, and Edison J. Trickett, PhD (Vol. 8(2), 1991). *"A thoughtful and thought-provoking summary of ethical issues related to intervention programs and community research." (Betty Tableman, MPA, Director, Division of Prevention Services and Demonstration Projects, Michigan Department of Mental Health, Lansing) Here is the first systematic and focused treatment of the ethical implications of primary prevention practice and research.*

Career Stress in Changing Times, edited by James Campbell Quick, PhD, MBA, Robert E. Hess, PhD, Jared Hermalin, PhD, and Jonathan D. Quick, MD* (Vol. 8(1), 1990). *"A well-organized book. . . . It deals with planning a career and career changes and the stresses involved. " (American Association of Psychiatric Administrators)*

Prevention in Community Mental Health Centers, edited by Robert E. Hess, PhD, and John Morgan, PhD* (Vol. 7(2), 1990). *"A fascinating bird's-eye view of six significant programs of preventive care which have survived the rise and fall of preventive psychiatry in the U.S." (British Journal of Psychiatry)*

Protecting the Children: Strategies for Optimizing Emotional and Behavioral Development, edited by Raymond P. Lorion, PhD* (Vol. 7(1), 1990). *"This is a masterfully conceptualized and edited volume presenting theory-driven, empirically based, developmentally oriented prevention. " (Michael C. Roberts, PhD, Professor of Psychology, The University of Alabama)*

The National Mental Health Association: Eighty Years of Involvement in the Field of Prevention, edited by Robert E. Hess, PhD, and Jean DeLeon, PhD* (Vol. 6(2), 1989). *"As a family life educator interested in both the history of the field, current efforts, and especially the evaluation of programs, I find this book quite interesting. I enjoyed reviewing it and believe that I will return to it many times. It is also a book I will recommend to students." (Family Relations)*

A Guide to Conducting Prevention Research in the Community: First Steps, James G. Kelly, PhD, Nancy Dassoff, PhD, Ira Levin, PhD, Janice Schreckengost, MA, AB, Stephen P. Stelzner, PhD, and B. Eileen Altman, PhD* (Vol. 6(1), 1989). *"An invaluable compendium for the prevention practitioner, as well as the researcher, laying out the essentials for developing effective prevention programs in the community. . . . . This is a book which should be in the prevention practitioner's library, to read, re-read, and ponder." (The Community Psychologist)*

Prevention: Toward a Multidisciplinary Approach, edited by Leonard A. Jason, PhD, Robert D. Felner, PhD, John N. Moritsugu, PhD, and Robert E. Hess, PhD* (Vol. 5(2), 1987). *"Will not only be of intellectual value to the professional but also to students in courses aimed at presenting a refreshingly comprehensive picture of the conceptual and practical relationships between community and prevention." (Seymour B. Sarason, Associate Professor of Psychology, Yale University)*

Prevention and Health: Directions for Policy and Practice, edited by Alfred H. Katz, PhD, Jared A. Hermalin, PhD, and Robert E. Hess, PhD* (Vol. 5(1), 1987). *Read about the most current efforts being undertaken to promote better health.*

The Ecology of Prevention: Illustrating Mental Health Consultation, edited by James G. Kelly, PhD, and Robert E. Hess, PhD* (Vol. 4(3/4), 1987). *"Will provide the consultant with a very useful framework and the student with an appreciation for the time and commitment necessary to bring about lasting changes of a preventive nature." (The Community Psychologist)*

Beyond the Individual: Environmental Approaches and Prevention, edited by Abraham Wandersman, PhD, and Robert E. Hess, PhD* (Vol. 4(1/2), 1985). *"This excellent book has immediate appeal for those involved with environmental psychology . . . likely to be of great interest to those working in the areas of community psychology, planning, and design." (Australian Journal of Psychology)*

Prevention: The Michigan Experience, edited by Betty Tableman, MPA, and Robert E. Hess, PhD* (Vol. 3(4), 1985). *An in-depth look at one state's outstanding prevention programs.*

Studies in Empowerment: Steps Toward Understanding and Action, edited by Julian Rappaport, Carolyn Swift, Robert E. Hess, PhD* (Vol. 3(2/3), 1984). *"Provides diverse applications of the empowerment model to the promotion of mental health and the prevention of mental illness." (Prevention Forum Newsline)*

Aging and Prevention: New Approaches for Preventing Health and Mental Health Problems in Older Adults, edited by Sharon P. Simson, Laura Wilson, Jared Hermalin, PhD, and Robert E. Hess, PhD (Vol. 3(1), 1983). *"Highly recommended for professionals and laymen interested in modern viewpoints and techniques for avoiding many physical and mental health problems of the elderly. Written by highly qualified contributors with extensive experience in their respective fields." (The Clinical Gerontologist)*

Strategies for Needs Assessment in Prevention, edited by Alex Zautra, Kenneth Bachrach, and Robert E. Hess, PhD* (Vol. 2(4), 1983). *"An excellent survey on applied techniques for doing needs assessments. . . It should be on the shelf of anyone involved in prevention." (Journal of Pediatric Psychology)*

Innovations in Prevention:, edited by Robert E. Hess, PhD, and Jared Hermalin, PhD* (Vol. 2(3), 1983). *An exciting book that provides invaluable insights on effective prevention programs.*

Rx Television: Enhancing the Preventive Impact of TV, edited by Joyce Sprafkin, Carolyn Swift, PhD, and Robert E. Hess, PhD* (Vol. 2(1/2), 1983). *"The successful interventions reported in this volume make interesting reading on two grounds. First, they show quite clearly how powerful television can be in molding children. Second, they illustrate how this power can be used for good ends." (Contemporary Psychology)*

Early Intervention Programs for Infants, edited by Howard A. Moss, MD, Robert E. Hess, PhD, and Carolyn Swift, PhD* (Vol. 1(4), 1982). *"A useful resource book for those child psychiatrists, paediatricians, and psychologists interested in early intervention and prevention." (The Royal College of Psychiatrists)*

Helping People to Help Themselves: Self-Help and Prevention, edited by Leonard D. Borman, PhD, Leslie E. Borck, PhD, Robert E. Hess, PhD, and Frank L. Pasquale* (Vol. 1(3), 1982). *"A timely volume . . . a mine of information for interested clinicians, and should stimulate those wishing to do systematic research in the self-help area." (The Journal of Nervous and Mental Disease)*

Evaluation and Prevention in Human Services, edited by Jared Hermalin, PhD, and Jonathan A. Morell, PhD* (Vol. 1(1/2), 1982). *Features methods and problems related to the evaluation of prevention programs.*

Educating Students to Make-a-Difference: Community-Based Service Learning

Joseph R. Ferrari
Judith G. Chapman
Editors

Educating Students to Make-a-Difference: Community-Based Service Learning has been co-published simultaneously as *Journal of Prevention & Intervention in the Community*™, Volume 18, Numbers 1/2 1999.

The Haworth Press, Inc.
New York • London

Educating Students to Make-a-Difference: Community-Based Service Learning has been co-published simultaneously as *Journal of Prevention & Intervention in the Community*™, Volume 18, Numbers 1/2 1999.

The development, preparation, and publication of this work has been undertaken with great care. However, the publisher, employees, editors, and agents of The Haworth Press and all imprints of The Haworth Press, Inc., including The Haworth Medical Press and Pharmaceutical Products Press, are not responsible for any errors contained herein or for consequences that may ensue from use of materials or information contained in this work. Opinions expressed by the author(s) are not necessarily those of The Haworth Press, Inc.

Cover design by Thomas J. Mayshock Jr.

The Haworth Press, Inc., 10 Alice Street, Binghamton, NY 13904-1580 USA

Library of Congress Cataloging-in-Publication Data

Educating students to make-a-difference : community-based service learning / Joseph R. Ferrari, Judith G. Chapman, editors.
     p. cm.
    "Co-published simultaneously as Journal of prevention & intervention in the community, volume 18, numbers 1/2 1999."
    Includes bibliographical references and index.
    ISBN 0-7890-0684-7 (alk. paper)
    1. Student service–United States. 2. Student volunteers in social service–United States. 3. College students–United States. 4. Community and college–United States. I. Ferrari, Joseph R. II. Chapman, Judith G. III. Journal of prevention & intervention in the community.
LC220.5.E38 1999
378'.015'0973–dc21
                                       99-10982
                                         CIP

INDEXING & ABSTRACTING

Contributions to this publication are selectively indexed or abstracted in print, electronic, online, or CD-ROM version(s) of the reference tools and information services listed below. This list is current as of the copyright date of this publication. See the end of this section for additional notes.

- *Abstracts of Research in Pastoral Care & Counseling*
- *Behavioral Medicine Abstracts*
- *BUBL Information Service. An Internet-based Information Service for the UK higher education community.*
- *Child Development Abstracts & Bibliography*
- *CNPIEC Reference Guide: Chinese National Directory of Foreign Periodicals*
- *EMBASE/Excerpta Medica*
- *Family Studies Database (online and CD/ROM)*
- *HealthPromis*
- *IBZ International Bibliography of Periodical Literature*
- *Mental Health Abstracts (online through DIALOG)*
- *National Center for Chronic Disease Prevention & Health Promotion (NCCDPHP)*
- *National Clearinghouse on Child Abuse & Neglect*
- *NIAAA Alcohol and Alcohol Problems Science Database (ETOH)*
- *OT BibSys*
- *Psychological Abstracts (PsycINFO)*
- *Referativnyi Zhurnal (Abstracts Journal of the All-Russian Institute of Scientific and Technical Information)*
- *RMDB DATABASE (Reliance Medical Information)*

(continued)

- *Social Planning/Policy & Development Abstracts (SOPODA)*

- *Social Work Abstracts*

- *Sociological Abstracts (SA)*

- *SOMED (social medicine) Database*

- *Violence and Abuse Abstracts: A Review of Current Literature on Interpersonal Violence (VAA)*

Special Bibliographic Notes related to special journal issues (separates) and indexing/abstracting:

- indexing/abstracting services in this list will also cover material in any "separate" that is co-published simultaneously with Haworth's special thematic journal issue or DocuSerial. Indexing/abstracting usually covers material at the article/chapter level.
- monographic co-editions are intended for either non-subscribers or libraries which intend to purchase a second copy for their circulating collections.
- monographic co-editions are reported to all jobbers/wholesalers/approval plans. The source journal is listed as the "series" to assist the prevention of duplicate purchasing in the same manner utilized for books-in-series.
- to facilitate user/access services all indexing/abstracting services are encouraged to utilize the co-indexing entry note indicated at the bottom of the first page of each article/chapter/contribution.
- this is intended to assist a library user of any reference tool (whether print, electronic, online, or CD-ROM) to locate the monographic version if the library has purchased this version but not a subscription to the source journal.
- individual articles/chapters in any Haworth publication are also available through the Haworth Document Delivery Service (HDDS).

Educating Students to Make-a-Difference: Community-Based Service Learning

CONTENTS

SERVICE AS LEARNING: STUDENT, FACULTY, AND COMMUNITY OUTCOMES

ABOUT THE EDITORS

Joseph R. Ferrari, PhD, is Associate Professor in the Department of Psychology at DePaul University in Chicago, Illinois, and Editor-in-Chief of *Journal of Prevention & Intervention in the Community* since 1995. Dr. Ferrari received his PhD from Adelphi University, with a concentration in experimental social-personality psychology. In addition to his interest in mainstream social psychological issues, such as persuasion, attribution theory, and altruism, he has developed several lines of research in social-community psychology. His community research includes the psychological sense of community, caregiver stress and satisfaction, behavior analysis applications to community issues, and volunteerism and community service.

Judith G. Chapman, PhD, is Dean, College of Arts and Sciences at Saint Joseph's University, Philadelphia, Pennsylvania, and Reviewer for *Journal of Prevention and Intervention in the Community*. Dr. Chapman received her PhD in Social Psychology from Syracuse University. Her research interests include small group processes, social cognition, social anxiety/blushing, volunteerism, and media influence. Dr. Chapman has been recognized twice with the Merit Award for Excellence in Teaching, and has taught a service learning course entitled "The Psychology of Violence and Aggression." She is the author/co-author or editor of more than thirty articles, papers, workshops, and symposia.

An Introduction
to Community-Based
Service Learning (CBSL)

Judith G. Chapman

Saint Joseph's University

Joseph R. Ferrari

DePaul University

Service learning, an educational experience that affords students the opportunity to apply experiences gained in helping others to their understanding of material learned in the classroom, is an increasingly popular mode of education in high schools, colleges, and universities throughout the United States. Surveys suggest that one quarter of all high school students are involved in service-learning courses (Independent Sector, 1990), and over one-half of all college students engage in some form of volunteer activity (Levine, 1994). Many institutions of higher education have adopted programs supporting service-learning as a direct reflection of their stated missions to raise awareness of, and bring resources to the solution of social problems. As funding of governmental service programs continues to decline, it becomes apparent that we will have to rely on our citizenry to meet the needs of underserved populations. Service-learning programs and courses are considered viable ways of promoting a strong sense of social responsibility in students (Boyer, 1994; Markus, Howard, & King, 1993).

In addition to promoting moral and social values, studies have begun to document the educational benefits of service-learning opportunities (Markus

[Haworth co-indexing entry note]: "An Introduction to Community-Based Service Learning (CBSL)." Chapman, Judith G., and Joseph R. Ferrari. Co-published simultaneously in *Journal of Prevention & Intervention in the Community* (The Haworth Press, Inc.) Vol. 18, No. 1/2, 1999, pp. 1-3; and: *Educating Students to Make-a-Difference: Community-Based Service Learning* (ed: Joseph R. Ferrari, and Judith G. Chapman) The Haworth Press, Inc., 1999, pp. 1-3. Single or multiple copies of this article are available for a fee from The Haworth Document Delivery Service [1-800-342-9678, 9:00 a.m. - 5:00 p.m. (EST). E-mail address: getinfo@haworthpressinc.com].

et al., 1993; Miller, 1994), as well as benefits to personal and professional growth (Ellis, 1993; Ferrari & Geller, 1994; Giles & Eyler, 1994). Some institutions are beginning to pursue outcomes assessment of service-learning in an effort to determine whether the espoused value of service-learning is realized in practice (Driscoll, Holland, Gelmon, & Kerrigan, 1996). The studies included in this special volume cover a range of issues related to service-learning, addressing the "who," "why," and "so what" of service-learning experiences. We believe that collectively these studies provide important summaries of the value of service-learning not only for student volunteers, but for the communities they serve.

The studies presented in the first section, *Learning to Serve: Predispositions and Motivations,* focus on student motivations and predispositions for community service across a variety of student populations. Who are student volunteers and why do they donate their time and energies in service to others? Stukas and his colleagues suggest that children are more likely to be positively predisposed to service if they had strong parental models for service, with a stronger effect of parental modeling for girls than for boys. Gender differences are apparent across student populations of included studies; seventh grade girls are more predisposed to service than same-aged boys (Stukas et al.) and differences in motivations between genders appear among college students (Chapman & Morley) and medical students (Switzer, Switzer, Stukas, & Baker). The impact of mandatory service on attitudes and the likelihood of future volunteerism is addressed (Stukas et al.), as well as comparisons between the motives of students who are mandated to serve and those who volunteer to serve (Ferrari et al.), and between volunteers and nonvolunteers (Chapman & Morley; see also Gardner & Baron, next section). Two studies address possible change in the importance of motivations for service as a function of volunteer activity and on the satisfaction of student volunteers (Chapman & Morley; and Ferrari et al.). These studies have implications for selection and retention of student volunteers (Clary, Snyder, & Ridge, 1992; Omoto & Snyder, 1990).

The second section, *Service as Learning: Student, Faculty, and Community Outcomes,* moves beyond the "who" and "why" of student volunteers to questions of the impact of service-learning on students, faculty, and the community. These studies collectively suggest the positive impact that service-learning experiences have on academic performance as perceived by students (Gardner & Baron; Keys, Hernandez, Johnson, & Weslock; McKenna & Rizzo; Primavera; Reeb, Sammon, & Isackson; Rowe & Chapman) and by faculty (Rowe & Chapman). Studies provide indications of the positive impact of service-learning on students' perceptions of personal growth, particularly on level of self-esteem and self-efficacy (McKenna & Rizzo; Primavera, Rowe & Chapman; also see Ferrari et al. in Section 1), and problem-solving and leadership skills (Rowe & Chapman). Further evidence from these studies suggests that students and faculty believe that as a result of service, students have a greater awareness of social issues (Keys et al.; Primavera; Rowe & Chapman), a stronger sense of social responsibility (McKenna & Rizzo; Reeb et al.), and a greater appreciation of diversity (Keys et al.; Primavera). Students are not the only ones to benefit from service-learning. Faculty indicate the value of teaching service-learning courses (Rowe & Chapman) and positive outcomes for communities are apparent (Keys et al.; Reeb et al.).

The studies presented here on service-learning theoretically advance our knowledge and understanding of an important and valued social behavior. We would hope that they stimulate further research to aid in recruitment and retention of student volunteers and service-learning outcomes.

REFERENCES

Boyer, E. L. (1994, March 9). Creating the new American college. *The Chronicle of Higher Education*, A48.

Clary, E. G., Snyder, M., & Ridge, R. (1992). Volunteers' motivations: A functional strategy for the recruitment, placement, and retention of volunteers. *Non-Profit Management and Leadership*, 2(4), 333-350.

Driscoll, A., Holland, B., Gelmon, S., & Kerrigan, S. (1996). An assessment model for service-learning: Comprehensive case studies of impact on faculty, students, community, and institution. *Michigan Journal of Community Service Learning*, 3, 66-71.

Ellis, J. R. (1993). Volunteerism as an enhancement to career development. *Journal of Employment Counseling*, 30, 127-132.

Ferrari, J. R., & Geller, E. S. (1994). Developing future care-givers by integrating research and community service. *The Community Psychologist*, 27, 12-13.

Giles, D. E., & Eyler, J. (1994). The impact of a college community service laboratory on students' personal, social, and cognitive outcomes. *Journal of Adolescence*, 17(4), 327-329.

Independent Sector (1990). Volunteering and giving among American teenagers 14 to 17 years of age. *Finding from a National Survey Independent Sector*, Washington, DC.

Levine, A. (1994). Service on campus. *Change*, (July/August), 4-5.

Markus, G. B., Howard, J., & King, D. C. (1993). Integrating community service and classroom instruction enhances learning: Results from an experiment. *Educational Evaluation and Policy Analysis*, 15(4), 410-419.

Miller, J. (1994). Linking traditional and service-learning courses: Outcome evaluations utilizing two pedagogically distinct models. *Michigan Journal of Community Service Learning*, 1(1), 29-36.

Omoto, A. M., & Snyder, M. (1990). Basic research in action: Volunteerism and society's response to AIDS. *Personality and Social Psychology Bulletin*, 16(1), 152-165.

LEARNING TO SERVE: PREDISPOSITIONS AND MOTIVATIONS

Parental Helping Models, Gender, and Service-Learning

Arthur A. Stukas, Jr.
Galen E. Switzer
Mary Amanda Dew
Jeanne M. Goycoolea
Roberta G. Simmons

University of Pittsburgh

SUMMARY. Students may be predisposed to benefit from mandatory service-learning programs based on their gender and upon whether their parents serve as models of helping. The role of each of these variables was examined in a survey of seventh grade students (n = 86) who were required to complete service during the school year. Results dem-

Address correspondence to: Arthur A. Stukas, Jr., University of Northern Colorado, Department of Psychology, Greeley, CO 80639.

The authors regret that Roberta G. Simmons passed away before this manuscript was published.

[Haworth co-indexing entry note]: "Parental Helping Models, Gender, and Service-Learning." Stukas, Arthur A. Jr. et al. Co-published simultaneously in *Journal of Prevention & Intervention in the Community* (The Haworth Press, Inc.) Vol. 18, No. 1/2, 1999, pp. 5-18; and: *Educating Students to Make-a-Difference: Community-Based Service Learning* (ed: Joseph R. Ferrari, and Judith G. Chapman) The Haworth Press, Inc., 1999, pp. 5-18. Single or multiple copies of this article are available for a fee from The Haworth Document Delivery Service [1-800-342-9678, 9:00 a.m. - 5:00 p.m. (EST). E-mail address: getinfo@haworthpressinc.com].

onstrated that girls felt more positively about the specific program and were more likely to intend to help in the future than boys. Students with parental helping models were also more likely to intend to help in the future. Girls with parental models were more likely to have altruistic self-images than girls without parental models whereas the presence of parental helping models had no effect on boys' altruistic self-image. These results are discussed with regard to socialization of prosocial behavior in both boys and girls. *[Article copies available for a fee from The Haworth Document Delivery Service: 1-800-342-9678. E-mail address: getinfo@haworthpressinc.com]*

Service-learning programs may serve several functions for society. For one, these programs can cement bonds between educational institutions and the communities in which they reside by providing help and support to those in need and by facilitating interactions between students and members of the community who might not otherwise have contact. Moreover, as our society moves toward a greater degree of decentralization in government, the need for volunteers to provide social services becomes greater. Practically speaking, then, an important function of service-learning programs is actually to put volunteers to work to meet the needs of the community.

Yet, such programs are also clearly designed to help the participants themselves; another function of service-learning programs is to provide educational and psychological benefits to students. Many service-learning programs give students specific opportunities to apply or to observe principles learned in the classroom outside in the community. For example, political science lessons can be made concrete for students through participation in relevant community service (Markus, Howard, & King, 1993). Other programs, that are not aligned with specific course content, have also demonstrated significant benefits for students. Switzer, Simmons, Dew, Regalski, and Wang (1995) found improvements in self-esteem and school involvement (as well as declines in depressive affect and problem behavior) for students–especially boys–who engaged in service-learning, as compared to students who did not.

Finally, service-learning programs are also designed to promote the internalization of prosocial values and attitudes by students (see Sobus, 1995). It is clearly in the community's best interest to impress upon students the need for altruistic behavior; however, mere participation in service may not achieve this goal (Kendall, 1991). Thus, most programs include components (such as daily journals) that elicit critical reflection about the service experience from students. As Clary, Snyder, and Stukas (in press) note, this use of post-action reflection is consistent with social psychological theorizing about the internalization of values and attitudes (e.g., Bem, 1972). When volunteers are encouraged to reflect on and to frame their actions in terms of a broad prosocial values system, they may be led to perceive themselves as "people who help" and thus to develop an altruistic self-image, based on their own behavior. This altruistic self-image, combined with increased knowledge about how to help others, is predicted to lead to increases in rates of future volunteerism by these students. Indeed, Charng, Piliavin, and Callero (1988) have shown that continued experience as a blood donor can lead to a "role-person merger" during which the role of blood donor becomes an integrated and central part of the self-concept, and donating becomes habitual and routine.

Of course, the internalization of prosocial values and attitudes by students is probably not accomplished entirely by service-learning programs. One usually thinks of parents as the chief socialization agents for children, and parents who promote prosocial behavior and attitudes may have significant effects on their children's tendencies to help. As Rushton (1976) pointed out, observational learning from models (particularly powerful and/or nurturant models, such as parents) may play a role in the internalization of prosocial values. Indeed, many researchers have shown that parental helping models do influence the internalization of prosocial values and attitudes. For example, Clary and Miller (1986) presented evidence that telephone volunteers engaged in crisis-counseling who grew up with parents who modeled helping were more likely to remain as volunteers throughout the length of their contracts than volunteers who had not had parental helping models. Similarly, Rosenhan (1970) and Oliner and Oliner (1988) noted that committed Civil Rights activists and rescuers of Jews in Nazi-occupied Europe were more likely to report the significant influence of their parents and of modeling of helping than were matched comparison groups, respectively.

Thus, students with parental helping models may be predisposed to respond well to service-learning programs and to benefit more from them than students without parental helping models. Staub (1992) suggested that parents who model helping behavior for their children and who engage in "natural socialization" (by guiding children to help others) enable children to better learn by doing, or, in other words, to internalize prosocial values and attitudes through active helping. Staub also summarized his own work on the transmission of prosocial values and reported a strong gender difference such that girls who were led to help others were more likely to continue helping in the future than boys who were led to help. Staub speculated that some acts of kindness may be seen by boys as inconsistent with the masculine image they are trying to adopt. Indeed, gender differences in prosocial behavior have frequently been reported (see Rushton, 1976) and may be the result of differential socialization for boys and girls; that is, learning to be nurturant and altruistic may be more frequently a part of the normal socialization process for girls than for boys (Eagly, 1987).

The question at hand, then, is given students' participation in school service-learning programs, do students' gender and the presence of parental helping models influence the outcomes that are expected from such programs? Based on the evidence summarized above, students (especially girls) with parents who volunteer should benefit most from service-learning. Specifically, in a sample of seventh graders who participated in mandatory service-learning, we hypothesized that students would show greater internalization of prosocial values and attitudes (as represented by greater intentions to help in the future and stronger altruistic self-images) if they had parental helping models and if they were girls. We also expected that girls and/or students with parental helping models would enjoy the experience of service-learning more and be more strongly in favor of such required programs than students without parental helping models and/or boys.

METHOD

Participants

As part of the 1992-1993 school year curriculum, seventh graders at a New York City metropolitan area junior high school were randomly assigned either to participate in community service or to serve as control participants. Switzer et al. (1995) previously examined differences between the 134 students who served and the 104 students who did not; in the present study we focused only on those students who were assigned to service. Parents of these students were sent letters requesting informed consent for their children to complete our survey; the parents of 19% of the students (n = 26) did not respond or declined to allow their children to participate. Twenty-two students (16% of original sample) did not complete the study. The current study concerns the 86 students (64% of original sample) who fulfilled the service option and our survey.[1] Most students in the final sample were 11 or 12 years of age (99%), Christian (58%), and from two-parent families (86%); 52% of the students were girls. The sample was 41% White with sizable Asian (28%) and Hispanic (19%) minorities. This sample was comparable to the general population of the school.

Parental Helping Models. To sort students according to our principal independent variable, students were asked the following question: "Do either of your parents spend time helping other people outside of their regular jobs? For example, do they help elderly neighbors, volunteer at soup kitchens, or perform some other activity?" Students responded on a 4-point scale ranging from "not at all" to "yes, a lot." They were categorized into two groups, students *with* parental helping models and students *without* parental helping models, by dividing the scale at the midpoint; 47% of students said that their parents helped "a little" or "a lot" and 53% said that their parents helped "not at all" or "not very much."

Procedure

The Service Program. Students in our study were randomly assigned to participate in the required service-learning program, beginning in October 1992 and continuing through May 1993. Based on their class schedules, students participated in either a formal version of this requirement (N = 26) or an informal version (N = 60). In the formal program, students were required to serve either as (a) tutors (n = 19) for younger students or students for whom English was not the primary language, or (b) companions and helpers (n = 7) at a local senior center, where they worked on craft projects and designed oral history projects with the residents. These students spent roughly one hour a week in these helping activities over the course of seven months.

The remaining students participated in the helping program more informally by selecting their own service projects from a list of suggestions provided by the school that included helping the family, school, neighborhood, social service organizations, religious organizations, environmental organizations, the community, or persons in need. Some of these students also chose to meet their commitment by either tutoring (n = 9) or working with the elderly (n = 4). Other students took added responsibilities at school, such as counseling students in detention or acting as a teacher's aide (n = 10). The majority of students in the informal program (n = 36) met their requirement by performing a variety of tasks, supervised by their parents, ranging from babysitting to serving meals at a church soup kitchen.[2] The school principal sent a letter to parents of students in the informal program that stated that he believed "helping or serving others should be a significant and on-going part of life." The letter went on to describe several helping options, and to ask parents to assist in facilitating productive activities for their children. Students' activities were monitored and forms that certified their participation were signed by parents, teachers, organization staff, or, in some cases, the recipients themselves.

Self-report questionnaires were administered to students at the end of the school year after they had completed their service. Students completed an approximately 40-minute questionnaire in the school cafeteria on 1 of 2 consecutive days. Although students were also asked about extracurricular activities and about other issues related to their school lives, only those measures relevant to the current study will be described here (please see Switzer et al., 1995, for results of other measures).

Dependent Measures

On the questionnaire, students reported their attitudes toward, and intentions for, helping others, as well as their specific attitudes about the helping requirement. To ensure that items with differing response scales were weighted equally, each item was standardized before being averaged with other items to form a scale.

Altruistic Self-Image. The degree to which students saw themselves as altruists was measured by a four-item scale created for this study, based on Piliavin's work with blood donors (Piliavin & Callero, 1991). Examples of items are "I really don't have any clear feelings about helping others" and "Helping others is an important part of who I am." Students answered on a 9-point scale ranging from "strongly agree" to "strongly disagree" (Cronbach's alpha for the current study was 0.69).

Commitment to Help Others. Students indicated their commitment by answering three items, again based on Piliavin and Callero (1991), including "Would you be disappointed in yourself if you did not help others in the future?" (1 = "no," 2 = "yes") and "Would you describe yourself as a person who often helps others?" (1 = "no," 3 = "often helps"); alpha = 0.67.

Better Person Scale. The degree to which students felt like better persons after having helped others was measured by a three-item scale developed by Simmons, Klein, and Simmons (1977), in their work with kidney donors, and modified for use with adolescents. Examples of items are "Do you somehow feel like a better person after having taken part in the school helper program?" (1 = "no," 2 = "yes"), and "When you think about your participation in the school helper program, have you felt . . ." (1 = "not at all proud," 3 = "very proud"); alpha = 0.66.

Self-Impression of Help Quality. Students responded to: "I could have worked a little harder at helping others through the helper program this year" on a 4-point scale, ranging from "strongly agree" to "strongly disagree."

Attitudes Toward Required Service. Two items were combined to serve as an indicator of students' attitudes toward service requirements at their school. These items were "Students should be required to participate in helper programs at their schools" (1 = "strongly disagree," 4 = "strongly agree") and "How likely would you be to help others if your school did not require it?" (1 = "very unlikely," 4 = "very likely"). Higher scores indicated that students felt that they would help even if it was not required and that requirements in schools are a good idea. These two items were correlated at $r = .39$, $p < .01$.

Attitudes Toward Specific Helping Activities. Students rated their helping activities on three 9-point scales with the following endpoints: "very fun" to "not very fun," "boring" to "interesting," and "good way to spend time" to "waste of time." Responses to these items formed a scale (alpha = 0.81) with higher scores indicating positive attitudes.

RESULTS

Overview

Initially, we compared students who met their service requirement by participating in formal versus informal activities. These two groups did not differ significantly in the presence of parental helping models (formal = 48% with models, informal = 47% with models), or in gender composition (formal = 63% boys, informal = 49% boys). Independent t-tests were conducted with each of the six dependent variables; all differences were nonsignificant (p > .10). On the basis of the high degree of similarity between the programs on our variables of interest, we concluded that the two groups of students should be combined for the remaining analyses.

We grouped our dependent measures into three pairs that appeared to represent meaningful conceptual sets, moving from general attitudes about helping to more specific reactions to the actual program and its activities. The first pair included Commitment to Helping and Altruistic Self-Image; these two scales were correlated at $r = .46$ and measured students' general orientation toward altruistic behavior. As a whole, the seventh graders reported being committed to helping ($M = 4.63$ out of a possible 8; $SD = 1.31$), and possessing altruistic self-images ($M = 21.21$ out of 36; $SD = 6.87$). The second pair of scales included the Better Person scale and the Self-Impression of Help Quality item; these scales were significantly correlated at $r = .30$ and focused on students' feelings after having helped others. In general, students felt like better people after helping ($M = 5.58$ out of 9; $SD = 1.55$), and that they had provided high-quality help ($M = 2.60$ out of 4; $SD = 0.71$). The third pair of scales included Attitudes Toward Required Service and Attitudes Toward Specific Helping Activities; these scales were correlated at $r = .37$ and assessed students' attitudes toward aspects of the helping program that were mostly outside of their control. In general, the seventh graders in the program reported believing in the use of community service requirements ($M = 5.78$ out of 8; $SD = 1.29$), and feeling positively toward their required helping activities ($M = 13.52$ out of 21; $SD = 4.36$). Table 1 provides a complete listing of standardized and unstandardized means and standard deviations for each scale by key study groups.

We performed three separate Multivariate Analyses of Variance (MANOVAs), one for each of the three sets of dependent variables, with gender and parental model status as between-subjects variables. Thus, each MANOVA incorporated a 2 × 2 design with a linear combination of two scales as dependent variables. Univariate F-tests were examined when significant multivariate effects were present. See Table 2 for the complete MANOVA results. It is important to note that these univariate tests take advantage of shared variance among the dependent variables; more than one test may be

TABLE 1. Unstandardized and Standardized Means and Standard Deviations for Six Helping-Related Outcome Variables as a Function of Gender and the Presence or Absence of Parental Helping Models

| Measure[a] | Scale | Student Has Parental Helping Models | | | |
| | | No | | Yes | |
		Boy	Girl	Boy	Girl
Altruistic Self-Image	raw (4 to 36)	20.93(6.30)	17.89(5.40)	21.00(6.71)	24.91(7.48)
	z	−0.08(0.65)	−0.39(0.55)	−0.07(0.69)	+0.33(0.77)
Commitment to Helping	raw (3 to 8)	4.54(1.45)	4.79(1.13)	4.63(1.12)	5.59(1.14)
	z	−0.21(0.87)	−0.05(0.67)	−0.14(0.67)	+0.44(0.67)
Better Person	raw (3 to 9)	4.89(1.63)	6.71(1.05)	5.00(1.25)	6.11(1.24)
	z	−0.40(0.82)	+0.55(0.50)	−0.27(0.62)	+0.23(0.63)
Self-Impression of Help Quality	raw (1 to 4)	2.41(0.84)	2.65(0.49)	2.84(0.69)	2.53(0.77)
	z	−0.23(1.14)	+0.10(0.66)	+0.36(0.93)	−0.07(1.04)
Attitudes Toward Required Service	raw (2 to 8)	5.50(1.44)	6.25(1.24)	5.50(1.15)	6.56(1.03)
	z	−0.21(0.94)	+0.25(0.83)	−0.22(0.73)	+0.46(0.67)
Attitudes Toward Specific Activities	raw (3 to 21)	12.46(5.42)	14.31(3.82)	12.61(2.20)	15.56(4.16)
	z	−0.26(1.06)	+0.11(0.75)	−0.24(0.43)	+0.34(0.81)

[a]Higher scores indicate more positive or favorable outcomes.

significant because they are measuring common traits or behaviors (see Tabachnick & Fidell, 1996).

Altruistic Orientation

The first MANOVA involved two dependent variables: Commitment to Helping and Altruistic Self-Image. As demonstrated by the Wilks' Lambda criterion, the combined dependent variables were significantly affected by parental helping models and by the interaction of gender and parental helping models; the main effect of gender was marginally significant.

A significant univariate main effect of parental helping models was found for the Altruistic Self-Image scale and a marginally significant main effect was found for the Commitment to Helping scale. Students with parental helping models were more likely to have altruistic self-images (M z-score =

TABLE 2. Multivariate Analysis of Variance Results as a Function of Parental Helping Models and Gender

Altruistic Orientation	Parental Helping Models F	Gender F	Interaction F
Multivariate Test	3.38*	2.90#	3.05*
Altruistic Self-Image	6. 29*	0.09	6.08*
Commitment to Helping	2.96#	5.32*	1.74

Feelings About Having Helped	Parental Helping Models F	Gender F	Interaction F
Multivariate Test	0.93	12.98**	1.89
Better Person	------	22.68**	------
Self-Impression of Help Quality	------	0.05	------

Attitudes Toward Program	Parental Helping Models F	Gender F	Interaction F
Multivariate Test	0.27	5.74**	0.24
Attitudes Toward Required Service	------	8.87**	------
Attitudes Toward Specific Activities	------	5.95 *	------

Note. For analyses involving the Altruistic Orientation set, the degrees of freedom for the F tests were as follows: Multivariate test (2,83), Univariate tests (1,84); for the Feelings About Having Helped set: Multivariate test (2,77), Univariate tests (1,78); and for the Attitudes Toward Program set: Multivariate test (2,69), Univariate tests (1,70).
#p < .10; *p < .05; **p < .01.

+0.14) and to be committed to helping (*M z*-score = +0.17) than students without parental helping models, who were less likely to have altruistic self-images (*M z*-score = −0.20) and less likely to be committed to helping (*M z*-score = −0.14). A significant univariate effect of gender was found for the Commitment to Helping Scale. Boys (*M z*-score = −0.17) were less likely to be committed to helping than girls (*M z*-score = +0.21). No significant univariate effect of gender was found for Altruistic Self-Image.

Finally, a significant interaction of parental helping models and gender was found only for Altruistic Self-Image. Simple effects tests revealed that girls with parental helping models were much more likely to have altruistic self-images than girls without parental helping models (*M z*-scores: +0.33 vs. −0.39, *t*(39) = 3.39, *p* < .01), whereas boys with parental helping models were no different in their altruistic self-images from boys without parental helping models (*M z*-scores: −0.07 vs. −0.08, *t*(45) < 1). Figure 1 shows a graphical representation of this interaction.

FIGURE 1. Standardized altruistic self-image scale means as a function of gender and the presence or absence of parental helping models.

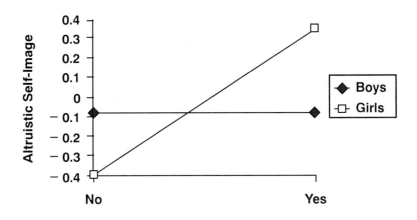

Parental Helping Models

Feelings About Having Helped

The second MANOVA included the following two dependent variables: Self-Impression of Help Quality, and the Better Person Scale. As demonstrated by the Wilks'Lambda criterion, the combined dependent variables were affected significantly only by gender (see Table 2). There was no significant effect of parental models or an interaction of models by gender. A significant univariate effect of gender was found for the Better Person Scale only. Girls were more likely to feel that they were better people after helping than boys (M z-scores: +0.38 vs. − 0.34). There was not a significant univariate effect of gender for Self-Impression of Help Quality.

Attitudes Toward Program

The third MANOVA included Attitudes Toward Required Service and Attitudes Toward Specific Helping Activities as dependent variables. As demonstrated by the Wilks' Lambda criterion, the combination of these two variables was significantly affected by gender alone (see Table 2). Both Attitudes Toward Required Service and Attitudes Toward Specific Helping Activities showed significant univariate effects of gender. Girls were more likely to feel positively toward required service programs than boys

(*M* z-scores: +0.36 vs. − 0.21) and to hold more positive attitudes toward their helping activities than boys (*M* z-scores: +0.22 vs. − 0.25).

DISCUSSION

As predicted, positive outcomes after a mandatory service-learning program were associated with both gender and the presence of parental helping models. Primarily, girls were more likely to have internalized the value of helping than were boys, as evidenced by the multivariate main effect for the set of Altruistic Orientation measures, composed of Altruistic Self-Image and Commitment to Helping. Girls were also more likely to feel positively about the quality of help they had delivered and about themselves as persons after helping than boys, as shown by the multivariate main effect for gender on the set of dependent variables measuring Feelings About Having Helped. Finally, girls also were more likely to feel positively toward both the activities they had just completed, and the institution of requirements for community service more generally, than boys, as suggested by the strong multivariate main effect for the set of variables reflecting Attitudes Toward Program.

The strong influence of gender on reactions to service-learning may reflect differences in the socialization of boys and girls with regard to helping others, in general, or to community service, in particular. Indeed, Miller (1994) reported a strong gender effect in reactions to the idea of mandatory community service such that female high school students viewed required programs far more favorably than male high school students. Miller suggested that girls may focus on the motives underlying the institution of a requirement (i.e., to get more students to engage in service) whereas boys may focus on the procedural justice, or fairness, of the method itself (i.e., the compulsory nature of the program). Boys, therefore, may experience greater psychological reactance (e.g., Brehm & Brehm, 1981) to the removal of their freedom to choose whether or not to engage in service than girls; this reactance may reduce boys' likelihood to volunteer in the future. This suggests that our strong gender difference could be limited to the effects of *mandatory* service-learning programs rather than the effects of more voluntary service programs. (We should note, however, that, in our previous study of this group (Switzer et al., 1995), boys who participated in service did show improvements in self-esteem and other variables unrelated to helping motivation, as compared to boys who were not randomly assigned to participate; thus, boys did benefit from service although not in intentions to help.)

Turning to the impact of having parental helping models, students with such role models were, on the whole, more likely to be committed to future helping and more likely to have altruistic self-images. This modeling effect may have resulted from both active and passive circumstances in the family.

Thus, some parents who help may actively facilitate critical reflection about community service by their children, perhaps through family discussions, and they may actually engage in service with their children. These activities could serve to better internalize the values of a caring society in these young people. Alternately, our main effect of parental helping models may be a more passive effect, due to the mere presence of helping parents, that prepared students for "learning by doing" in their service program. In this view, regardless of parents' efforts to internalize values in children, their "good example" may be enough to predispose their children to benefit from service-learning. Of course, given the post-test nature of our data, we cannot be certain whether children with parental models entered our program with greater commitment to helping than children without models or whether the program helped children of models to specifically internalize that commitment.

Finally, the presence of parental helping models also interacted with gender to affect responses to the Altruistic Self-Image scale. Girls with parental helping models were far more likely to have altruistic self-images than girls without parental helping models, whereas the presence or absence of models seemed to make no difference for boys' self-images. Because girls are more likely to be guided and socialized to be nurturant and altruistic in our culture (e.g., Eagly, 1987), perhaps they are more sensitive to the modeled help of their parents. Girls with parents who do help may find society's message to them reinforced, but girls with parents who do not help may have that message undercut. For boys, the cultural message seems to be that nurturance may not be masculine (e.g., Staub, 1992), thus, without cultural support for an altruistic self-image, the presence or absence of parental helping models may have no effect on boys.

In retrospect, we would have liked to have obtained more detail about students' parents and their helping activities. For example, it would be helpful to know whether fathers and/or mothers served as helping models to aid our interpretation of the above interaction with gender. Additionally, some data on the ways parents may have modeled helping and sought to internalize prosocial values in their children would have been helpful. Similarly, more detail about students' actual helping activities would have allowed a more fine-grained analysis of how specific helping activities may differentially affect outcomes. Clearly, a longitudinal study that focuses upon the ways in which parents model helping, the way service-learning is presented to students, the details of the specific activities engaged in by students, and the subsequent effects on student outcomes is needed.

Nevertheless, our results suggest two things. First, a thorough examination of the apparent resistance of boys to altruistic behavior must be undertaken. Perhaps enticing boys into service-learning without the use of requirements is the answer. Clary et al. (in press) suggest that this may be done by focusing potential volunteers on the personal benefits available to them through helping. Second, the assistance of parents in this socialization effort is necessary. It is even possible that parents who do not actively model altruistic behavior could have negative effects on their children's self-image as helpful people; this appears to be of concern for girls, in particular. If we are serious about increasing altruism in our society, we must work together to provide as many examples of prosocial behavior to our children, both boys and girls, as we can.

NOTES

1. Fourteen students failed to complete the attitudes component of the survey. These students did not significantly differ from those who completed all of the measures in the proportion who had parental helping models (complete, 45.8%; incomplete 50.0%) or in their proportions of boys and girls (complete, 57.5% boys; incomplete, 35.7% boys).

2. In order to investigate whether the type of helping task completed affected student outcomes, specific helping activities were categorized as either: (a) tutoring (33%); (b) service to the elderly (13%); (c) other school-related activities (12%); or (d) informal one-time tasks (42%). There were no significant differences in the gender composition or in the proportions of students with parental helping models by task type. Additionally, six one-way ANOVAs (for each of the central dependent variables) also demonstrated nonsignificant effects for task type.

REFERENCES

Bem, D. (1972). Self-perception theory. In L. Berkowitz (Ed.), *Advances in experimental social psychology* (Vol. 6, pp. 1-61). New York: Academic Press.

Brehm, S. S., & Brehm, J. (1981). *Psychological reactance: A theory of freedom and control.* New York: Academic Press.

Charng, H., Piliavin, J. A., & Callero, P. L. (1988). Role identity and reasoned action in the prediction of repeated behavior. *Social Psychological Quarterly, 51*, 303-317.

Clary, E. G., & Miller, J. (1986). Socialization and situational influences on sustained altruism. *Child Development, 57*, 1358-1369.

Clary, E. G., Snyder, M., & Stukas, A. A. (in press). Service-learning and psychology: Lessons from the psychology of volunteers' motivations. In R. G. Bringle & D. K. Duffy (Eds.), *Collaborating with the community: Psychology and service-learning.* Washington, DC: American Association of Higher Education.

Eagly, A. (1987). *Sex differences in social behavior: A social role interpretation.* Hillsdale, NJ: Lawrence Earlbaum.

Kendall, J. C. (1991). Combining service and learning: An introduction for cooperative education professionals. *Journal of Cooperative Education, 27*, 9-26.

Markus, G., Howard, J., & King, D. (1993). Integrating community service and classroom instruction enhances learning: Results from an experiment. *Educational Evaluation and Policy Analysis, 15*(4), 410-419.

Miller, F. (1994). Gender differences in adolescents' attitudes toward mandatory community service. *Journal of Adolescence, 17*, 381-393.

Oliner, S., & Oliner, P. (1988). *The altruistic personality: Rescuers of Jews in Nazi Europe.* New York: Free Press.

Piliavin, J. A., & Callero, P. L. (1991). *Giving blood: The development of an altruistic identity.* Baltimore: Johns Hopkins University Press.

Rosenhan, D. (1970). The natural socialization of altruistic autonomy. In J. Macauley & L. Berkowitz (Eds.), *Altruism and helping behavior* (pp. 251-268). New York: Academic Press.

Rushton, J. P. (1976). Socialization and the altruistic behavior of children. *Psychological Bulletin, 83*, 898-913.

Simmons, R. G., Klein, S. D., & Simmons, R. L. (1977). *Gift of life: The social and psychological impact of organ transplantation.* New York: Wiley.

Sobus, M. S. (1995). Mandating community service: Psychological implications of requiring prosocial behavior. *Law and Psychology Review, 19*, 153-182.

Staub, E. (1992). The origins of caring, helping, and nonaggression: Parental socialization, the family system, schools, and cultural influence. In P. M. Oliner, S. P. Oliner, L. Baron, L. A. Blum, D. L. Krebs, & M. Z. Smolenska (Eds.), *Embracing the other: Philosophical, psychological, and historical perspectives on altruism.* New York: New York University Press.

Switzer, G. E., Simmons, R. G., Dew, M. A., Regalski, J. M., & Wang, C. (1995). The effect of a school-based helper program on adolescent self-image, attitudes, and behavior. *Journal of Early Adolescence, 15*(4), 429-455.

Collegiate Service-Learning:
Motives Underlying Volunteerism
and Satisfaction with Volunteer Service

Judith G. Chapman
Richard Morley

Saint Joseph's University

SUMMARY. The present investigation assessed the volunteer motives among male and female college students and examined whether levels of these motives changed after participation in service. First year students (33 in a course with a service-learning experience, 27 in the same course without this component) and upper-class students (n = 25) in upper-level service-learning courses were compared. Results suggested that Values and Understanding motives were most important, and Protective and Social motives were least important across college volunteers. Females rated Values, Understanding, and Self-Esteem motives more important than did males, and service-learning students rated Values and Understanding motives more important than did nonservice-learning students. Values, Protective, and Social motives were predictive of overall satisfaction with the service experience. Results have implications for recruitment, satisfaction, and retention of student volunteers. *[Article copies available for a fee from The Haworth Document Delivery Service: 1-800-342-9678. E-mail address: getinfo@haworthpressinc.com]*

Address correspondence to: Judith Chapman, Saint Joseph's University, 5600 City Avenue, Philadelphia, PA 19131 (E-mail: jchapman@sju.edu).

This research was supported in part by a grant from Pennsylvania Campus Compact.

[Haworth co-indexing entry note]: "Collegiate Service Learning: Motives Underlying Volunteerism and Satisfaction with Volunteer Service." Chapman, Judith G., and Richard Morley. Co-published simultaneously in *Journal of Prevention & Intervention in the Community* (The Haworth Press, Inc.) Vol. 18, No. 1/2, 1999, pp. 19-33; and: *Educating Students to Make-a-Difference: Community-Based Service Learning* (ed: Joseph R. Ferrari, and Judith G. Chapman) The Haworth Press, Inc., 1999, pp. 19-33. Single or multiple copies of this article are available for a fee from The Haworth Document Delivery Service [1-800-342-9678, 9:00 a.m. - 5:00 p.m. (EST). E-mail address: getinfo@haworthpressinc.com].

19

A national survey conducted in 1989 by Independent Sector (1990), a coalition of 650 nonprofit organizations, estimated that over 98 million adults volunteered some of their time to nonprofit organizations at an estimated worth of over $170 billion. Further, volunteers provided services to over 40,000 volunteer organizations (Kotter, 1982, as cited in Unger, 1991). As the U.S. government's role in providing social services continues to decline, the need for volunteers to provide those services will continue to increase (Romero, 1986). Recently, President Clinton (Presidents' Service Summit, April 1997, Philadelphia) called for a commitment to encouraging volunteerism and targeted, in particular, programs aimed at teaching the value of volunteer service to the youth of America.

People engage in volunteer activity for a variety of reasons. For example, some volunteers believe that helping others is a responsibility shared by all members of civilized societies, implying a social responsibility norm (Crandall & Harris, 1976). Others volunteer because they believe that volunteering in a certain capacity will enable them to secure the skills and experience that is required for employment in a particular profession (Ellis, 1993). Although service to one's community is most likely interpreted as a form of altruism (Fitch, 1987; Frisch & Gerrard, 1981), the motivational bases for volunteer activity can vary greatly from individual to individual, and for one individual over time. Evidence suggests that both altruistic and self-serving motives explain volunteerism (Fitch, 1987; King, 1984; Steiner, 1984), and Serow (1991) suggests that motivations for volunteering are "complex and variable, potentially encompassing a mixture of self-regarding and other-regarding forces" (p. 546). Gillespie and King (1985) found that reasons given for volunteering vary between age groups, with those in their mid-thirties or older indicating more altruistic motives relative to those in their late teens to mid-thirties, who indicated more self-serving motives aimed at enhancing career skills or opportunities.

Clary and Snyder and their colleagues (Clary & Snyder, 1991; Clary, Snyder & Ridge, 1992; Clary et al., in press; Clary, Snyder, & Stukas, 1996; Omoto & Snyder, 1990, 1991) have proposed and employed a functional approach (Katz, 1960) to the study of volunteerism. This functional approach focuses on the individual motives and needs that are fulfilled by engaging in volunteer service (Clary et al., 1992; Snyder, 1993). It emphasizes the diversity of motives that underlie volunteer behavior and can have important implications for methods that are used by organizations to advertise for, select, and retain volunteers (Clary & Snyder, 1991; Clary et al., in press; Omoto & Snyder, 1990). The same volunteer behavior can serve different functions for different individuals, and the same volunteer behavior of one individual can serve multiple functions. Further, this approach recognizes that individual motives may interact with volunteer experiences to determine the effectiveness of service and satisfaction with service (Clary et al., in press; Omoto & Snyder, 1990).

Clary et al. (1992) have identified six major motives for volunteer service. Expression of the *Values* motive allows one to act on the belief of the importance of helping others. A need to understand others, oneself in relation to those served, or organizations whom one serves underlies the *Understanding* motive. The *Career* motive is expressed when volunteer behavior enhances career opportunities or skills, or allows one to develop career contacts, whereas the *Social* motive reflects a need to engage in service to meet the normative expectations of others who are valued or held in high esteem. The *Self-Esteem* motive is indicated when service provides an opportunity for one to feel good about himself or herself or to feel needed or important as a result of engaging in service. Finally, the *Protective* motive addresses a need to relieve or escape negative or aversive feelings (for example, loneliness or guilt) through service to others. Results of studies that have assessed these motives for volunteering have indicated the importance of multiple motives for any one individual and considerable variability in motives rated most and least important between individuals (Clary & Snyder, 1991; Clary et al., 1992; Clary, Snyder, & Stukas, 1996; Omoto & Snyder, 1991). Studies have suggested that matching motives to volunteer activities results in higher performance ratings and greater satisfaction with service (Clary & Snyder, 1991; Clary et al., in press) and that some motives are better predictors of continued service than others (Clary et al., in press).

The purposes of the present investigation were: (a) to assess the motives that underlie volunteerism in a traditional-aged college population; (b) to determine whether motives change as a function of participation in service [motives that sustain volunteerism may not be identical to those that encourage it initially (Smith, Ready, & Baldwin, 1972)]; and (c) to determine whether or not motives are accurate predictors of satisfaction with service. With the cooperation of the Director of our university-wide Service-Learning Program, a sample of incoming students enrolled in freshman service-learning courses was obtained along with a comparable control group. In addition, a second sample comprised of upper-level students enrolled in upper-level courses with a service-learning component was obtained. Courses taken in our Service-Learning Program require that students spend a minimum of 3-4 hours in community service each week. The objective of the program is to provide traditional-age college students with the opportunity to integrate volunteer service with the learning experience of the classroom. This integration is aimed at deepening the students' understanding of responsibility to the communities in which they live and corresponds to the Ignatian ideal of our Jesuit institution of teaching our students to "be people for others."

Although this study is primarily exploratory in nature, it was expected that there would be an increase in the relative importance of the Social motive, particularly for incoming students as they acclimated to college life and became familiar with other students and the professor of the service-learning class. No predicted changes in importance were predicted for other motives. Of additional interest was whether gender differences in the relative importance of motives would be evidenced. Social role theory (Eagly, 1987; Eagly & Crowley, 1986) suggests that females are more likely to engage in helping behavior as a function of their greater tendency to nurture relative to males, and that this gender difference may be a function of early socialization processes (Eagly, 1987). Previous research has found that volunteers who are motivated by the Values function score highly on measures of nurturance and social responsibility (Omoto & Snyder, 1991). Therefore, it might be expected that the Values motive would be a more important motive for females relative to males.

It is expected that motives for service will predict satisfaction with service (Clary & Snyder, 1991; Clary et al., in press). As such, the relative importance of the motivational bases for volunteering for service-learning may ultimately be a useful tool in recruitment and retention of students in the service-learning program. The relationship between any particular motive and satisfaction with service may indicate what features of service are or are not meeting the needs of those who volunteer.

METHOD

Participants and Procedure

Data were collected across two consecutive semesters, Fall (1994) and Spring (1995). Questionnaire data were obtained at the beginning and end of each semester. Questionnaires were distributed to 48 service-learning and 104 nonservice-learning students at the beginning of the fall semester in their regularly scheduled classes. A return envelope was provided with instructions that questionnaires could be returned to the professor of the class or to the office of the investigator. Response rates to the initial survey were 100% for the service-learning students, and 70% for the follow-up measure taken at the end of the semester. This resulted in 60 students in the fall sample: 33 enrolled in service-learning courses (upper-level Spanish and Moral Philosophy), and 27 enrolled in other sections of the same course that did not have a service-learning component. All of these students were incoming, first-year students.

Questionnaires were handed out to 42 upper-level service-learning students during the spring semester, all enrolled in upper-level specialty classes

(Fine Arts and Sociology). The response rate for the initial questionnaire was 60%, and four of those students failed to complete the follow-up survey, resulting in 25 students in the spring sample. Because these were upper-level specialty courses, no comparable nonservice-learning courses were available from which to draw a control group.

Materials

Demographic Questionnaire. The initial questionnaire packet contained a student demographic sheet which asked students to indicate their gender, age, race, religion, geographic location of their home, whether they attended public or private high school, high school GPA, and college major. They were asked if they had volunteered their time in the past (nonpaid work of a volunteer nature) and if so, how many hours per week, on average. They were asked to provide a brief description of their volunteer service. Three questions asked about the educational background of their parents and a gross estimate of parental income. One question asked students to describe their general views using a 9-point scale with endpoints labeled 'conservative' and 'liberal.' Finally, they were asked to indicate whether "business and industry, churches/foundations/nonprofit organizations, government, needy people themselves, average citizens like myself, or a total restructuring of society" would best solve the problems of the poor, the homeless, and other needy groups, by circling any one option.

Volunteer Functions Inventory. At the beginning and end of the semester, Clary et al.'s (1992) Volunteer Functions Inventory (VFI) was included in the questionnaire packets completed by participants. This 30-item questionnaire differentiates six "functions" of volunteerism by identifying the motives that volunteers seek to satisfy in volunteer work. Participants are asked to respond to each item on 7-point scales where 1 = not at all important/accurate for you; 7 = extremely important/accurate for you. Motive scores were obtained by summing values for respective subscale items, with higher scores indicating greater importance of that motive. Scale items have been shown to have high internal reliability ($\geq$ 0.80, Clary et al., 1992; Clary et al., in press), and acceptable test-retest reliabilities ($\geq$ 0.60, Clary et al., 1992). Subscale alpha levels obtained in the current study are presented in Table 1.

Social Desirability Scale. At the beginning of the semester students completed the Crowne-Marlow (1960) Social Desirability Scale (SDS), a 33-item scale which assesses need for avoidance of disapproval, with higher scores indicating a greater concern about the evaluations of others. Participants respond to all items by indicating whether it is true or false as it pertains to them. We included this measure to determine if responses to the VFI were impacted by self-presentational concerns of participants. Scale authors have shown the internal consistency of the SDS to range from 0.73-0.88, and

TABLE 1. Alpha Coefficients and Mean Scale Values on the Relative Importance of Volunteer Motives Across Student Samples and Overall Samples

Motives	Alpha	Student Samples			
		Fall, SL (n = 33)	Fall, NSL (n = 27)	Spring, SL (n = 25)	Overall (n = 85)
Values	0.81	5.82 (1.34)	5.14 (0.99)	6.10 (0.91)	5.67 (1.09)
Understanding	0.84	5.64 (1.28)	5.03 (1.03)	5.45 (1.31)	5.39 (1.23)
Self-Esteem	0.81	4.85 (1.42)	4.36 (1.39)	4.25 (1.41)	4.53 (1.42)
Career	0.86	4.04 (1.68)	4.45 (1.40)	4.47 (1.73)	4.29 (1.60)
Protective	0.79	3.75 (1.59)	3.44 (1.19)	3.02 (1.50)	3.45 (1.45)
Social	0.85	2.58 (1.56)	3.03 (1.41)	2.80 (1.41)	2.79 (1.31)

Note: Values in parentheses are standard deviations. SL = Service-learning sample; NSL = Nonservice-learning sample.

test-retest reliability from 0.84-0.88. Internal consistency of the SDS in the present study is 0.82.

Satisfaction Questionnaire. At the end of the semester, service-learning students completed a second questionnaire packet, and in addition to reassessing their motives for volunteering (VFI), a questionnaire assessed their satisfaction with service on six items: Overall satisfaction with their service experience, satisfaction with duties performed at the service site, satisfaction with amount of time spent in service per week, satisfaction with the level of interaction with clients at the site, satisfaction with level of interaction with staff members at the site, and satisfaction with the level of interaction with other volunteers at the site. They responded to these items on 9-point scales where 1 = Not at all Satisfied, and 9 = Very satisfied. Finally, they were asked to indicate whether they would take another service-learning course or recommend one to other students.

RESULTS

Demographic Characteristics of the Samples

The majority of the students across samples were Catholic (86%), Caucasian (84%) women (74%), from suburban households (68%), who attended private high schools (59%). These demographics reflect the general character of the population at this small, private school with the exception of gender. The percentage of women who participated each semester in the service-learning courses was appreciably greater than the population percentage (71% Fall, 84% Spring, when women comprise 53% of the student population).

The average age of samples was 19 (*SD* = 1.41; 18 in the Fall, 20 in the Spring). Most had a B+ average in high school (average GPA = 3.41, *SD* = 0.39) and enrolled in the college as Social Science (29%) or Humanities majors (28%). The majority of their parents have had, at minimum, some college (father, 98%; mother, 72%), and 67% come from households which have incomes above $60,000 per year. These students described themselves as slightly more liberal than conservative (*M* = 5.56 on a 9-point scale, *SD* = 2.16). The majority of service-learning students have volunteered in the past (70%), on average, two hours per week (*M* = 2.29, *SD* = 1.94), whereas the majority of nonservice-learning students have not volunteered (74%). Those nonservice-learning students who have, volunteered on averaged less than one hour per week (*M* = 0.82; *SD* = 1.55). The most frequent response given to the question of who best can solve the problems of the needy was 'average citizens' (26%). However, interesting distinctions emerge between subsamples. Whereas responses of incoming service-learning students in the Fall sample reflected a belief that average citizens should respond to the problems of the needy (42%), the most frequent responses of incoming nonservice-learning students was that the needy should solve their own problems (26%) or should be assisted by a restructuring of society (39%). The opinions of upper-class service-learning students were more evenly distributed across options: The plight of needy should be addressed by the government (20%), average citizens (20%), and social restructuring (24%).

Correlations between the SDS and each subscale of the VFI were not significant for any of the three subsamples, consistent with findings from previous research (Clary et al., 1992; Ferrari et al., this issue).

Relative Importance of Motives for Volunteering

Of primary interest in this study was the relative importance of motives for students in the sample (see Table 1). Although the range of values across motives suggests that each was considered to be relatively important by some students in each subsample (the smallest range was 3.4 units on a 7 point scale), the *Values* and *Understanding* motives appeared to be most important within and across subsamples. Again, these motives suggest a need to act on one's personal values and beliefs about the importance of helping others and to understand those served and oneself in relation to those served, respectively. The *Protective* and *Social* motives appeared to be least important, suggesting that, in general, these students were not motivated by a need for approval from others, nor did they volunteer in order to alleviate aversive feelings (perhaps, loneliness and/or guilt). It should be emphasized, however, that drawing generalizations within and across subsamples blurs the relative importance of motives at the individual level. Although the *Values* and *Understanding* motives were rated as most important generally, they were not rated as the most important motives by every individual in the sample.

Table 2 presents the frequency with which each of the six motives were rated as most important by each subsample and by the entire sample of 85. As can be seen, the *Social* and *Protective* motives were the only motives that were not rated as being most important by any participants in the sample. Overall, 54% of entire sample rated the *Values* motive as most important, 32% rated the *Understanding* motive as most important, 20% rated the *Career* motive as most important, and 12% rated the *Self-Esteem* motive as most important.

Independent *t*-tests were done to determine if there were any gender differences in rated importance of these motives. Table 3 presents means and standard deviations of motive ratings by gender. Women rated the *Values* ($t[31]= 2.81$, $p = .009$), *Understanding* ($t[31] = 2.01$, $p = .05$), and *Self-Esteem* ($t[31] = 2.19$, $p = .04$) motives significantly more important than men did in the Fall sample. The *n*'s for men in the nonservice-learning subsample and the upper-class spring sample were too small to do any reliable tests.

Independent *t*-tests compared the service-learning and nonservice-learning subsamples in the Fall sample to determine whether differences existed in relative importance of motives between the two groups. Significant differences emerged on the *Understanding* and *Values* motives ($t(58) = 1.99$, $p = .05$, and $t(58) = 2.45$, $p = .02$, respectively). In both cases, service-learning students rated these two motives as more important than did nonservice-learning students, although the overall ranks of these two motives did not differ between the two subsamples.

Change in the Relative Importance of Motives as a Function of Volunteering

The second purpose of the study was to determine whether the relative importance of motives changed as a function of the service-learning experience. Again, the reasons why an individual volunteers initially may be quite different from why that individual continues to volunteer. Table 4 presents these data. The overall importance of motives does not change with service, as evidence in this table. The ranks of motives are identical to those obtained before service.

To determine if the rated importance of individual motives changed as a result of service experience, *t*-tests compare pre- and post-service scores on

TABLE 2. Frequency of Motives Rated 'Most Important' for Each Sample and Overall Samples

Motives	Student Samples			
	Fall, SL (n = 33)	Fall, NSL (n = 27)	Spring, SL (n = 25)	Overall (n = 85)
Values Motive	20	12	14	46
Understanding Motive	16	6	5	27
Self-Esteem Motive	3	6	1	10
Career Motive	5	6	6	17
Protective Motive	0	0	0	0
Social Motive	0	0	0	0

Note: Some students had tying values for the most important of the six motives. In those cases, both motives were given a frequency count. SL = Service-learning sample, NSL = Nonservice-learning sample.

TABLE 3. Means of Motive Scale Values by Gender for the Fall Service-Learning Sample

Motives	Gender	
	Men (n = 13)	Women (n = 20)
Values	5.20 (1.13)	6.23 (0.97)
Understanding	5.11 (1.42)	5.98 (1.07)
Self-Esteem	4.22 (1.60)	5.26 (1.14)
Career	3.65 (1.64)	4.29 (1.70)
Protective	3.29 (1.82)	4.04 (1.39)
Social	2.46 (1.24)	2.66 (1.12)

Note: Values in parentheses are standard deviations.

each VFI subscale. No significant changes in the relative importance of individual motives emerged in the Fall sample. In the Spring sample, however, there was a significant increase in the importance of the *Social* motive following service ($t[18]$) = -2.63, $p = .02$), and a marginal increase in importance of the *Self-Esteem* motive, ($t[18]=1.77$, $p = .09$). Although the service experience did not reduce the importance of any other motives for

TABLE 4. Pre- and Post-Measure Mean Motive Scores by Service-Learning Samples

| Motives | Service-Learning Samples | | | |
| | Fall (n = 33) | | Spring (n = 25) | |
	Pre-SL	Post-SL	Pre-SL	Post-SL
Values Motive	5.82	5.92	6.10	6.05
	(1.14)	(1.19)	(0.91)	(0.85)
Understanding Motive	5.64	5.57	5.45	5.58
	(1.28)	(1.10)	(1.31)	(1.31)
Self-Esteem Motive	4.85	4.66	4.25[a]	4.73[a]
	(1.42)	(1.44)	(1.41)	(1.47)
Career Motive	4.04	3.54	4.47	4.85
	(1.68)	(1.33)	(1.73)	(1.50)
Protective Motive	3.75	3.54	3.02	3.11
	(1.59)	(1.16)	(1.50)	(1.38)
Social Motive	2.58	2.65	2.80[b]	3.35[b]
	(1.16)	(1.50)	(1.41)	(1.77)

[a]This difference between means is marginally significant, $p = .09$.
[b]These means are significantly different, $p = .02$.
Note: Values in parentheses are standard deviations. SL = Service-learning experience.

service, it had the impact of increasing concerns about meeting the expectations of others through service, and engaging in service in order to feel good about oneself or to feel important.

Motives as Predictors of Satisfaction with Service

The final purpose of the study was to determine whether motives predicted satisfaction with service. Satisfaction scores were regressed on motive scale values obtained following the service-learning experience. Statistical tests of the significance of motives as predictors of the satisfaction items are presented in Table 5. The *Values, Protective,* and *Social* motives significantly predicted overall level of satisfaction with service, and accounted for 43% of the variability in satisfaction scores. As the importance of acting on one's personal values and beliefs about helping others increased, overall satisfaction increased. The more service helped to alleviate aversive feelings, the more satisfaction experienced. The greater the value placed on meeting the expectations of others, the less satisfaction experienced. It appears that the service experience did not fulfill this particular motive.

The *Value* and *Social* motives were predictive of satisfaction with duties performed and accounted for approximately 20% of the variability in this satisfaction score. The more importance one placed on the need to act on

TABLE 5. Tests of the Significance of Motives as Predictors of Satisfaction with Volunteer Service for Each Satisfaction Item

Item	t	$p =$
Overall satisfaction with service:		
Value	3.78	.001
Understanding	− 1.04	.307
Protective	2.77	.009
Self-Esteem	− 1.24	.223
Career	1.60	.117
Social	− 2.91	.005
Satisfaction with duties performed:		
Value	2.16	.037
Understanding	− 0.43	.669
Protective	0.87	.389
Self-Esteem	− 0.77	.448
Career	1.40	.168
Social	− 1.95	.058
Satisfaction with time spent in service:		
Value	1.99	.053
Understanding	− 1.79	.081
Protective	0.07	.943
Self-Esteem	− 0.89	.380
Career	2.15	.038
Social	− 0.36	.723
Satisfaction with level of interaction with clients:		
Value	1.10	.278
Understanding	− 0.22	.828
Protective	0.43	.667
Self-Esteem	0.08	.936
Career	0.20	.844
Social	− 0.81	.425
Satisfaction with level of interaction with staff:		
Value	1.32	.193
Understanding	0.95	.350
Protective	1.15	.256
Self-Esteem	− 1.21	.234
Career	0.24	.809
Social	0.12	.903
Satisfaction with level of interaction with other volunteers:		
Value	− 1.21	.236
Understanding	2.37	.023
Protective	− 1.61	.116
Self-Esteem	0.79	.434
Career	0.47	.639
Social	− 0.09	.928

personal values and beliefs about helping others, the more satisfied one was with duties. The greater the value placed on meeting expectations of others, the less satisfaction experienced regarding duties performed.

The *Value* and *Career* motives were significant predictors of satisfaction with the amount of time spent in service per week. Together with the *Understanding* motive, which was marginally predictive, these motives accounted for approximately 18% of the variability in satisfaction with time spent in service. The greater the value placed on the need to act on personal values and beliefs about helping others, and the more one believed that service can enhance career skills, the more satisfied students were with time spent in service. The more important the motive to learn about and understand those served, the less satisfied students were with time spent in service. This latter finding suggests that students were not capable of satisfying this motive in the time available for service.

Motives were not predictive of satisfaction with level of interaction with clients or staff, but the *Understanding* motive was a significant predictor of satisfaction with level of interaction with other volunteers at the site, and accounted for approximately 19% of the variability in this satisfaction rating. The more important the motive to learn about and to understand those served (or oneself in relation to those served), the greater the satisfaction with the level of interaction with other volunteers at the site. Perhaps students found the opportunity for social comparison with other volunteers resulted in a consensual validation of their own feelings and impressions related to volunteering.

Only six percent of the Fall sample and four percent of the Spring sample indicated they would not be willing to take another service-learning course (33% of the Fall sample and 12% of the Spring sample did not respond to this item), and the majority of each (61% and 88%, respectively) said they would recommend a service-learning course to a friend.

CONCLUSIONS

The primary purpose of this study was to assess the motivations for volunteering in a collegiate population. In addition, we were interested in gender differences in the rated importance of motives, whether motives change as a function of service, and whether motives were predictive of satisfaction with the volunteer experience. The *Values* and *Understanding* motives appear to be most important overall, whereas the *Social* and *Protective* motives are least important to college student volunteers. In general, students are motivated by a need to act on their beliefs about the importance of helping others and a need for understanding those they serve, and not by needs for approval from others or needs to escape negative or aversive feelings. These findings are consistent with previous findings (Clary et al., in press; Omoto & Snyder, 1990) and coincide nicely with the purpose of the service-learning program; The integration of service and learning is aimed at deepening students' understanding of responsibility to the communities in which they live. By gaining a deeper understanding of the communities in which we live we are more able to act on our values that support beliefs about the importance of responsibility to others. Caution should be exercised in generalizing results to student populations in general, however. The demographics of this sample and the university community environment in which the students' study may be atypical of other student populations from larger and/or non-religiously affiliated institutions.

Service-learning students rated the *Values* and *Understandings* significantly more important to their volunteer activity than did nonservice-learning students. Since service-learning students were more likely to have volunteered previously, perhaps the benefits of volunteering include a greater appreciation for the opportunity to act on one's beliefs about the importance of helping others and an appreciation of greater understanding of those we serve and of ourselves in the process.

Women had higher ratings than men on each of the motive subscales, suggesting that they are more motivated to volunteer than males, in general. The *Values* motive was rated significantly more important by women than men, and indicates that women are more motivated by beliefs about the importance of volunteering their services relative to men (Clary et al., 1996). Consistent with social role theory (Eagly, 1987; Eagly & Crowley, 1986), females tend to place a higher value on nurturance and have a stronger sense of social responsibility than men as a result of socialization processes that emphasize these values more for girls than boys. Significant differences in ratings of the *Understanding* motive between genders, with women rating this motive as more important than men, suggests that women have a greater need to understand those they serve or themselves in the role of a volunteer. This, too, would be consistent with social role theory as women tend to be not only more nurturant, but more empathetic toward others. The present data suggest that women have a significantly greater need to maintain or enhance esteem through service relative to men, given their stronger motive to serve in order to feel needed or important, consistent with previous findings (Clary et al., 1996).

For upper-class service-learning students, there was increased importance placed on the *Social* motive following volunteer activity. Although this was expected for the incoming students in particular, perhaps more experienced students have learned the value of meeting others' expectations in a college setting relative to incoming students.

The final purpose of the study was to determine if motives were predictive of satisfaction with service. Others (Clary et al., 1992; Clary et al., in press; Omoto & Snyder, 1990) have suggested the value of matching motives with service activity to maximize satisfaction and retention of volunteers. The *Values* motive was particularly important to satisfaction in the present sample: To overall satisfaction, to satisfaction with duties performed, and to amount of time spent in service per week. It may be that a strong motive to act on one's belief about helping others allows one to appreciate the time spent in service and makes one more accepting of a wider range of duties that might be required in service. Of interest was the relationship between the *Social* motive and measures of satisfaction. The greater one's concern about meeting the expectations of others, the *less* satisfaction experienced. Perhaps concerns over the potential evaluation of one's performance contributed to a less than positive service experience for some students.

In addition to providing data that are important to our understanding of motives that underlie volunteerism in collegiate samples, these data may be useful to a director of a service-learning program. Not only would data on motives be important to the student selection process, but data could be useful in matching student volunteers with services expected at various sites in the community. They would also assist in predicting retention of volunteers once the service component of a course is ended. It is our hope to be able to match services required at various sites to student motives in an attempt to enhance their volunteer experiences. We need to provide students with opportunities to act on values related to helping others and to provide feedback that indicates that their service, regardless of the form it takes, is valuable. Since experiences gained through volunteer activity can determine one's attitude toward future volunteerism (Sharon, 1991), work is now underway to determine the relationship between different site characteristics and satisfaction of volunteers as factors that impact recruitment and retention.

REFERENCES

Clary, E. G., & Snyder, M. (1991). A functional analysis of altruism and prosocial behavior: The case of volunteerism. *Review of Personality and Social Psychology, 12*, 119-148.

Clary, E. G., Snyder, M., & Ridge, R. D. (1992). Volunteer's motivations: A functional strategy for the recruitment, placement, and retention of volunteers. *Nonprofit Management and Leadership, 2*, 333-350.

Clary, E. G., Snyder, M., Ridge, R. D., Copeland, J., Stukas, A. A., Haugen, J., & Miene, P. (in press). Understanding and assessing the motivations of volunteers: A functional approach. *Journal of Personality and Social Psychology.*

Clary, E. G., Snyder, M., & Stukas, A. A. (1996). Volunteers' motivations: Findings from a national survey. *Nonprofit and Voluntary Sector Quarterly, 25(4)*, 485-505.

Crandall, J. E., & Harris, M. D. (1976). Social interest, cooperation, and altruism. *Journal of Individual Psychology, 32*, 50-54.

Crowne, D. P., & Marlowe, D. (1960). A new scale of social desirability independent of psychopathology. *Journal of Counseling Psychology, 24*, 349-354.

Eagly, A. (1987). *Sex differences in social behavior: A social role interpretation.* Hillsdale, NJ: Lawrence Earlbaum.

Eagly, A., & Crowley, M. (1986). Gender and helping behavior: A meta-analytic review of the social psychological literature. *Psychological Bulletin, 100*, 283-308.

Ellis, J. R. (1993). Volunteerism as an enhancement to career development. *Journal of Employment Counseling, 30*, 127-132.

Fitch, R. T. (1987). Characteristics and motivations of college students volunteering for community service. *Journal of College Student Personnel*, September, pp. 424-430.

Frisch, M. B., & Gerrard, M. (1981). Natural helping systems: A survey of Red Cross volunteers. *American Journal of Community Psychology, 9*, 567-579.

Gillespie, D. F., & King, A. E. (1985). Demographic understanding of volunteers. *Journal of Sociology and Social Welfare, 12(4)*, 798-816.

Independent Sector (1990). *Giving and volunteering in the United States: Findings from a national survey.* Washington, DC: Author.

Katz, D. (1960). The functional approach to a study of attitudes. *Public Opinion Quarterly, 24*, 163-204.

King, A. E. (1984). Volunteerism participation: An analysis of the reasons people give for volunteering. *Dissertation Abstracts International, 45*, 5, 1528-A.

Omoto, A. M., & Snyder, M. (1990). Basic research in action: Volunteerism and society's response to AIDS. *Personality and Social Psychology Bulletin, 16*, 152-166.

Omoto, A. M., & Snyder, M. (in press). AIDS volunteers and their motivation: Theoretical issues and practical concerns. *Nonprofit management and Leadership.*

Romero, C. J. (1986). The economics of volunteerism: A review. In Committee on an Aging Society (Ed.), *Productive roles in an older society* (pp. 23-51). Washington, DC: National Academy Press.

Serow, R. C. (1991). Students and Voluntarism: Looking into the Motives of Community Service Participants. *American Educational Research Journal, 28*, 534-556.

Sharon, N. (1991). Fitting volunteers with tasks and creating tasks for volunteers: A look at the role of volunteers in a community context. *Journal of Volunteer Administration, 5*, 4-12.

Smith, D. H., Reddy, R. D., & Baldwin, B. R. (1972). Types of voluntary action: A definitional essay (pp. 159-195). In D. H. Smith, R. D. Reddy, & B. R. Baldwin (Eds.), *Voluntary Action Research.* Lexington, MA: D. C. Health & Company.

Snyder, M. (1993). Basic research and practical problems: The promise of a "functional" personality and social psychology. *Personality and Social Psychology Bulletin, 19*, 251-264.

Steiner, T. (1984). An investigation of motivational factors operative in prosocial volunteers. *Dissertation Abstracts International, 36*, 6B, 3130.

Unger, L. (1991). Altruism as a motivation to volunteer. *Journal of Economic Psychology, 12*, 71-100.

Community Volunteerism Among College Students and Professional Psychologists: Does Taking Them to the Streets Make-a-Difference?

Joseph R. Ferrari
Kristie Dobis
Eva I. Kardaras
Denise M. Michna
Jeremy M. Wagner

DePaul University

Sara Sierawski
Peggy Boyer

Benedictine University

SUMMARY. Across three different samples of young adults, volunteer motives were unrelated to social desirability but volunteer motives of

Address correspondence to: Joseph R. Ferrari, Department of Psychology, DePaul University, 2219 North Kenmore Avenue, Chicago, IL 60614-3504.

The authors are grateful for the assistance offered by Tom Drexler and Dan Theiss, DePaul University's Campus Ministry program, and George Michel and Lucinda Rapp, DePaul University's Psychology Department, for their cooperation and assistance in the data collection in these studies.

[Haworth co-indexing entry note]: "Community Volunteerism Among College Students and Professional Psychologists: Does Taking Them to the Streets Make-a-Difference." Ferrari, Joseph R. et al. Co-published simultaneously in *Journal of Prevention & Intervention in the Community* (The Haworth Press, Inc.) Vol. 18, No. 1/2, 1999, pp. 35-51; and: *Educating Students to Make-a-Difference: Community-Based Service Learning* (ed: Joseph R. Ferrari, and Judith G. Chapman) The Haworth Press, Inc., 1999, pp. 35-51. Single or multiple copies of this article are available for a fee from The Haworth Document Delivery Service [1-800-342-9678, 9:00 a.m. - 5:00 p.m. (EST). E-mail address: getinfo@haworthpressinc.com].

35

values with understanding, and esteem with protection, were positively related. In one study, college students enrolled in an education course requiring volunteerism at a community day care center were compared to students who fully volunteered their time at this site. There were no significant differences between groups in terms of self-reported volunteerism motives or desire for control. The second study involved college honor students who volunteered at a number of community sites as a part of a leadership program. These students reported greater satisfaction than stress over a 12-week period from their service, and there was no significant change in their volunteerism motives over time. In the third study, graduates of clinical and experimental doctoral programs in psychology claimed that their volunteer motive of acting on personal values was significantly related to a sense of optimism, and a feeling of empowerment in their personal lives and in the future of their community. *[Article copies available for a fee from The Haworth Document Delivery Service: 1-800-342-9678. E-mail address: getinfo@haworthpressinc.com]*

National attention within the American education system in recent years has focused on *service learning* which involves student's committing their time and talents as volunteers within the local community providing assistance to others. A recent survey of adolescents suggested that about one quarter of their high schools offered courses that required community service as part of the course work (Independent Sector, 1990). Service is a high school graduation requirement in 4% of public schools and in 14% of Catholic schools (Newmann & Rutter, 1983). College campus-based service, the focus of the present study, also has been of interest to administrators, involving about 60,000 volunteers each year (Youth Service American, 1988).

Educators consider the effects of community volunteerism as a way to promote civic responsibility and moral growth in students. Community service programs can be thought of as a primary prevention tool and a means of empowering "help-givers" (Moore & Allen, 1996). For example, Newmann and Rutter (1983) proposed that community service may aid the caregiver's development into competent, independent persons, and promotes the growth of reasoning skills, abstract and hypothetical thought, and problem-solving abilities. In addition, volunteering may increase one's self-esteem, self-worth, mastery over his/her life, dependability, leadership capabilities, personal sense of social responsibility, and getting along with others (Harrison, 1987; Kirby, 1989). In short, community service may increase a volunteer's personal perceptions of self-efficacy and empowerment (Ferrari & Geller, 1994; Ferrari & Jason, 1997a).

In reviewing the literature on volunteers working with persons with AIDS, Omoto and Snyder (1990; Snyder, 1993) described a set of volunteerism motives that they claimed were applicable to volunteers in general. They suggest that motives for volunteering were personal ("selfish") and other ("selfless") oriented, with individuals most likely driven by both orientations. These motives included: *values,* a personal feeling of obligation to help others; *understanding,* a desire to gain a better knowledge of a group of people or social phenomenon; *social,* a sense of civic concern or commitment to aid others; *career,* a way of gaining hands-on experiences that enhance one's occupational skills; *esteem,* a way of enhancing one's self-worth by aiding others; and, *protective,* a desire to prevent feelings of loneliness and isolation by getting involved in the service of others. Snyder and his colleagues (Snyder, 1993; Clary, Snyder, & Ridge, 1992) claim that most volunteers report the motives of values and understanding as their highest desires for assisting others.

The present study focused on examining the motives of community service volunteers from a number of settings that included their performing various activities. The first two studies included college students who either were required to perform community service ("mandatory volunteerism") or who simply donated their time and talents. These students were surveyed initially and again at either eight or fourteen weeks after starting their service experience. These volunteers were from different colleges and performed different types of services. The third study was a sample of young adults whose professional training included components of community awareness, and these persons were polled on their present community service motives. Besides volunteer motives, participants completed reliable and valid self-report measures that assessed a desire for control, psychological sense of community, caregiving stress and satisfaction, religious orientation, empowerment, and optimism. Taken together, these exploratory studies aimed to contribute additional support and clarification of the impact and origins of volunteer community service by students and professionals who are "working the streets."

Across all three studies it should be noted that participants completed Clary et al.'s (1992) *Volunteer Functions Inventory* (VFI), a 30-item, 7-point rating scale where respondents report how important or accurate each possible reason for volunteering is for them. For each participant, six scores were calculated that corresponded to the six different motivations (each with five items) that can be satisfied by volunteering. High scores reflected the importance of that motive to the respondent. The scale has good internal consistency and temporal stability, as well as construct and predictive validities (see Clary et al., 1992; Clary, Snyder, & Stukas, 1996). With the present samples, their coefficient alphas are presented below (Tables 1 to 3, respectively). This instrument was used in the present studies to assess the motives of young adults to community-service activities and to determine (Studies 1 and 2) whether these motives changed over time from "selfish" to more "self-less" reasons.

Also, each participant completed the well known Crowne-Marlowe's (1960) *Social Desirability Scale* (SD), a 33 item, unidimensional, true/false measure. Participants completed this scale, embedded among other items, in order to determine whether there were response biases toward socially appropriate responses to their survey. It was expected that VFI scores would not be significantly related to SD scores, consistent with other studies (see Clary et al., 1992). Nevertheless, we felt it important to include the SD scale with each study as a "control" over potential response set toward socially desirable answers.

Thus, the motives for volunteering by young adults involved in several volunteer settings were assessed in three studies. Each study was a separate project conducted under the supervision of the first author but with the direction of the other authors as either a Senior Honor's Thesis (Study 1), an Independent Study project (Study 2), or simply an experience at conducting a research project (Study 3). In order to provide a context for these studies, a brief introduction to each project is stated below.

STUDY 1

In this study, college students majoring in early education programs and servicing a local day care center were asked to complete the VFI and SD instruments, as well as a measure on the desire for control. It is possible that a person may use volunteerism as a way to control others who are in need of their help or care. Perhaps the actions of providing care strengthens the volunteer's self-esteem, and provide him/her some self-protection (i.e., relief) over negative or aversive feelings. To the extent that this is a factor involved in community-service, it seemed logical to expect the desire for control by an adult (student) volunteer to be strongest when the recipient for help was a youth needing care (such as a young child), someone who may be in a position of being relatively powerless in that "altruistic" situation. It was expected, then, that if volunteerism was related to a desire for control over others, scores on the control scale would be negatively related to the volunteer motive of self-esteem and positively related to the protection motive.

Students either did or did not receive course credit for their community-service at the day care center. Further, among these students, a sub-set of participants also were asked to complete all measures at an eight-week follow-up to determine whether changes in their volunteer motives occurred over time. These individuals also completed a measure of the psychology sense of community, in order to assess whether a communal sense was established over time among individuals who provided care. The present study, therefore, provided an opportunity to compare the volunteer motives and characteristics of participants who were in a mandatory program for community-service with those who were more intrinsically motivated for service. These assessments permitted a closer examination of the desire for control over others and the motives for time and talents in volunteerism.

Method

Participants and Setting. There were 36 women (*M* age = 20.9, *SD* = 3.6 years old) majoring in an early education program at an urban, medium-size, private university in the midwest who participated in this project by providing community-service at a local day care center for children between the age of three to five years old. Most participants were Caucasian (47.2%), Roman Catholics (58.3%), and upper division students (55.6%). A number of these students (*n* = 16) were persons who volunteered their time as a way to gain relevant experience, while another group of students (n = 10) were persons enrolled in an internship course receiving credit for volunteering at the same day care center.

The day care setting included children from low income families whose parent(s) worked and the child was in attendance for the working hours of the day, usually most week days. The facility was located in a middle-class, urban setting within easy commute from the university for students. The center had a long term arrangement with the university that permitted students to serve as volunteers who provided services such as teaching preschool skills, providing play activities, and general care and supervision. Participants reported at least two weekly visits with the day care center, working on average three hours per visit along with three other volunteers from the university.

Psychometric Measures and Procedures. Each participants was approached by a female experimenter (KD) to volunteer a few minutes of their time to complete a demographic sheet and (in random order) the VFI, SD, and Burger and Cooper's (1979) 20-item, 7-point *Desire for Control* Scale. This scale has five subscales, namely: (a) *general desire* (5 items), a need to control others; (b) *decisiveness* (5 items), a preference for making decisions in order to gain control; (c) *preparation-prevention* (4 items), a desire to be well prepared before engaging in an activity; (d) *avoidance* (2 items), a need to avoid situations where one is dependent on others; and (e) *leadership* (4 items: reverse scored), a preference to have a superordinate role over the situation. The authors report that this research instrument has acceptable reliability and validity as a research tool.

Also, participants who completed a follow-up testing session completed Bishop, Chertok, and Jason's (1997) *Sense of Community* (SOC) inventory. Unlike other similar inventories that assess the physical characteristics of one's neighborhood, this new 30 item, 5-point scale assesses a person's psychological sense of: (a) *mission* (12 items), to evaluate the strength of the person's sense of a common mission; (b) *reciprocal responsibility* (12 items), to assess the person's commitment to offer assistance to others in the communal setting; and, (c) *disharmony* (6 items), to examine the level of disagreement between members. The authors reported good reliability (alpha $r = 0.75 - .096$), and the scale has construct validity with a communal-living setting involving self-help members (Bishop, Jason, & Ferrari, & Shu, in press).

Procedure. In this study, students either volunteered or were required through a course to commit their time and talents to a local community day care center. All participants signed and dated a consent form and then completed the set of inventories during their second week of volunteering at the center at the end of a day's volunteer session. The course was designed as a field experience practicum as a way to reinforce concepts presented in class. These students were required for their practicum course to meet weekly to discuss and reflect on experiences. All participants followed similar activities at the center, including reading to the children, setting-up play activities, and guiding and supervising preschool learning tasks. It took participants approximately 15 minutes to complete all measures. In addition, the mandatory volunteers were administered the set of inventories twice, once at the second week of class and again at the end of the eighth week of a ten week quarter.

Results and Discussion

Comparing Mandatory and Non-Mandatory Volunteers. Demographic and self-report inventory scores claimed at the initial testing session by participants in either the volunteer or mandatory groups were compared by t-tests for independent samples. There were no significant differences between these two groups on most of these measures. Therefore, no further comparisons between these two groups were performed.

Correlates Between Self-Reported Inventory Scores. Table 1 presents the mean score, coefficient alpha, and inter-scale score correlates between self-reported measures by the total sample of college student day care volunteers at the start of their volunteer experience. A visual inspection of the mean scores indicates that both understanding and values were the highest, and social and protective the lowest motives for volunteering. Participants also seemed to report a strong desire for decisiveness and were less likely to be avoiding situations requiring their control. Despite the fact that there were few participants in the present study and that some subscales included few items (2 or 4 items), the coefficient alphas suggest the data were fairly reliable with the present sample.

As noted from the table, participants indicated that social desirability was significantly negatively related with value motives for volunteering. This result suggests that for these respondents in the day care setting, social desirability was not significantly related to their motives to volunteer, and that no

TABLE 1. Mean Scores, Coefficient Alpha, and Zero-Order Correlates Between Self-Reported Psychometric Inventories in Study 1

MEASURE	M	(1)	(2)	(3)	(4)	(5)	(6)	(7)	(8)	(9)	(10)	(11)	(12)
VOLUNTEER FUNCTIONING MOTIVES:													
(1) social	12.36	[.73]											
(2) values	29.47	.27	[.62]										
(3) career	27.61	−.15	−.09	[.63]									
(4) understanding	30.39	.01	.45*	.42*	[.56]								
(5) esteem	20.19	.59*	.08	−.16	−.03	[.79]							
(6) protective	12.83	.56*	.13	.12	.04	.77*	[.76]						
DESIRE FOR CONTROL:													
(7) general	26.44	−.05	−.39*	.27	−.23	−.11	.04	[.55]					
(8) decisiveness	27.89	.19	.16	.04	.05	−.34*	.38*	−.02	[.75]				
(9) preparation/ prevention	22.92	.13	.16	−.17	.01	−.08	−.09	.14	−.19	[.51]			
(10) avoidance	7.33	.09	−.20	.22	−.17	−.10	.02	.48*	−.05	.19	[.55]		
(11) leadership	17.28	−.13	−.13	−.00	.18	−.08	−.04	.36*	.05	.19	.28	[.59]	
SOCIAL DESIRABILITY:													
(12)	17.71	.36*	−.24	−.02	−.13	−.03	−.12	.08	.05	.05	.21	−.09	[.79]

n = 36   *p* < .05

Note: Value in brackets is coefficient alpha.

response bias seemed to exist in the present data set. Among the volunteer motives significant and positive relations were obtained between social and both esteem and protective motives, and between understanding and both values and career motives. These results suggest that for these volunteers, living up to societal expectations to help others made them feel good and relieved negative emotions, and by satisfying a need to understand those being served (here, young children), participants were able to act on a belief that they should help others others while enhancing their own career skills. There also was a significant (and rather strong) positive relationship between esteem and protective motives, consistent with Clary et al.'s (1992) claim that volunteerism is motivated by a number of personal benefits to help others.

Moreover, there were significant negative relationships between a general desire for control and the volunteer motive of values. It seems that the more students volunteer for the purpose of acting on altruistic motives, the less likely they are operating from a need to control others or the situation. This result is particularly important since it demonstrates that young adults enrolled in an education program who offer their time and talents to help young children do not operate from a need to exert control over those children. Further, there were significant negative relationships between a decisive control desire and both esteem and protective volunteer motives. Therefore, this result again shows that personal motives reflecting a benefit for the care provider is not related to a need to exert control over the recipient of that service.

Initial and Follow-Up Comparisons on Self-Reported Inventory Scores by Mandatory Volunteers. Approximately eight weeks after beginning their quarter long volunteer experience, students enrolled in the education internship course ($n = 10$) were asked to again complete the VFI and DC scales, as well as the SOC scale for the first time. Of course, the small number of respondents for these evaluations limit the generalizability of results and warrants caution in interpretations. Nevertheless, a series of t-tests for paired samples (controlling for type 1 error) were performed to ascertain whether there were changes from initial and follow-up reported motives and desire for control. There was only one significant change across these measures: participants reported a significant increase in their social motive for volunteerism, from a mean of 9.4 ($SD = 4.9$) to 13.1 ($SD = 6.3$), t (9) = 2.76, $p < .02$. It seems that over time these students indicated they felt an increase in a need to meet the normative expectations of someone they hold in high regard (perhaps, their instructor).

In addition, zero-order correlates were conducted to assess whether the sense of community experienced by these students was related to their volunteer motives and/or desire for control. A sense of mission was significantly positively related to a desire for reciprocal responsibility among members ($r = .88$, $p < .001$), and negatively to preparedness in order to establish control over others ($r = -.65$, $p < .04$). Also, reciprocal responsibility was significantly negatively related to preparedness ($r = -.82$, $p < .001$), and disharmony in the community was significantly positively related to leadership ($r = .61$, $p < .05$). No other coefficients were significantly related, not surprising given the small number of respondents for analyses. Still, taken together it seems that over time volunteers working on separate but related community service develop a common bond and need to help each other. These sense of community factors do not seem to be related to their personal motives for volunteerism. A desire to control those receiving one's help was related to a low sense of common mission among one's group, and disharmony within that group was related to a desire to be a leader over others. Thus, it seems that volunteer motives are not related to need to control others (a drive for power). Mandatory and non-mandatory volunteers do not seem significantly different in their demographic or psychological make-up, and over a short period of time mandatory volunteers essentially don't report changes in their motives (although a sense of community may develop).

STUDY 2

A second study was conducted to build on Study 1. Participants again completed the VFI and SD inventories, to assess volunteer motives and social desirability tendencies. All students were enrolled in a mandatory program for campus leaders which included a semester long volunteer program. Students from a different institution were participants, permitting an examination of the generalizability of results of Study 1 to another population. Also, initial and follow-up evaluations were conducted over a 12 week period, to provide a longer time frame for potential change, and all participants were assessed at both testing sessions. In addition, participants in Study 2 completed a measure of caregiving stress and satisfaction, to ascertain their level of "burnout" from providing care to others, and a measure of religiousness, to examine whether a strong Judo-Christian sense of morality was a factor in their motives. As in Study 1, this second study was largely exploratory. Results were expected to be similar to those obtained in that first study.

Method

Participants and Settings. A total of 21 students (14 women, 7 men: *M* age = 19.7, *SD* = 1.5) enrolled at a small, private, suburban college in a sophomore-level leadership course, in which mandatory volunteer experiences were a course requirement, participated in this study. Most participants identified themselves as Christians (50%), stated they had been a volunteer in the past year (62%), and were natural or social science majors (66.6%).

Unlike Study 1, there was no constraint on the site for volunteering: students were encouraged to volunteer at any local community service organization. Because of the few number of persons included in this study, it was not possible to conduct a person X site evaluation. Nevertheless, participants volunteered to teach homeless children in an after school program (5), refurbish a home through Habitat-for-Humanity (4), offer study-mentoring aid to low income children (4), work as an aid in a local hospital and clinic (3), assist persons living in a center for the physically challenged (2), aid male inmates to learn effective communication skills (2), and tutor a bilingual child (1). Participants indicated that they currently were volunteering at their site for two months before the start of the course, visiting on average 2.5 times per month for 2.6 hours per visit.

Psychometric Measures. Besides completing the VFI and the SD inventories discussed above, Study 2 participants completed Ferrari, McCown, and Pantano's (1993) 14-item *Caregiver Scale*. This 7-point (1 = low; 7 = high) self-report inventory assessed the emotional experiences from working as a care provider to others. Two subscales comprise the inventory, including a personal *satisfaction* subscale (7 items: "Working [as a volunteer] is adding meaning to my life." "Helping [as a volunteer] is worthwhile to me.") and an emotional *stress* subscale (7 item: "Working with someone or people [as a volunteer] has exhausted me." "Helping someone [as a volunteer] has burned me out."). Ferrari et al. (1993) reported the satisfaction and stress scales were negatively related ($r = -0.50$), and that neither subscales was significantly related to social desirability. Both subscales were internally consistent and temporally stable. The inventory has been validated with target samples of health care, volunteer, and pastoral caregivers to persons with AIDS, as well as caregivers to physically disabled, elderly persons and homeless persons (Ferrari et al., 1993; Ferrari, Billow, Jason, & Grill, 1997; Ferrari & Jason, 1997b; Ferrari, Jason, & Salina, 1995). After six months of caring for persons with AIDS, caregivers' stress scores were found to be related to depression. Stress scores also were related to lower levels of knowledge about an illness, and satisfaction scores were related to perceived vulnerability to a physical illness.

Also, all participants completed Allport and Rosa's (1967) 20-item, 5-point *Religious Orientation Scale* (ROS). This well established measure distinguishes between intrinsically religious people (intrinsic subscale: 12 items; "I try hard to carry my religion over into all my other dealings in life.") who are genuinely committed to their faith from the more self-serving extrinsically religious person (extrinsic subscale: 8 items; "One reason for my being a congregation member is that such membership helps to establish me as a person in the community"). An impressive body of literature has indicated that individuals with an intrinsic faith are more psychologically adjusted than those persons who are extrinsically oriented toward religion (Donahue, 1985). Despite recent controversy over the utility of this measure (see Kirkpatrick & Hood, 1990), the ROS has been used extensively in research because it seems to be a reliable and valid inventory.

Procedure. All participants enrolled in an Honor's program to develop leadership skills were required to engage in a community-service project for 40 hours during a semester. These students meet weekly to discuss experiences and reflect on their role at the setting. During the second week of class, students were asked by a female experimenter to volunteer for a study that assessed their motives for volunteering. After signing and dating a consent form, participants completed all inventories, in random order. It took participants approximately 20 minutes to complete all items. At their service site, students engaged in a number of activities that reflected their time and talents, as noted above in the diversity of settings that they engaged. During the fourteenth week of the class, at the last group discussion session, the female experimenter asked students again to complete the set of inventories. All students in the class agreed to complete scales at the pre- and post-testing session.

Results

Table 2 presents the mean score, coefficient alpha, and inter-scale correlates between measures reported at the first testing session in Study 2. An inspection of the mean scores indicates that, consistent with Study 1, understanding and values were the highest and social and protective the lowest motives for volunteering. Participants also reported greater satisfaction than stress from being a volunteer, and tended to claim a greater external than internal religious desire. The coefficient alphas, given the small sample size, were good for research purposes. Social desirability scores were significantly positively related only to career motives for volunteering. This result suggests that responses to items in these surveys were not influenced by a need to state socially appropriate responses. Because of the small number of men in this sample, no statistical analyses were performed for gender comparisons on any of these measures.

Correlates Between Self-Reported Inventory Scores. Table 2 also shows the zero-order correlates between inventory scores used in Study 2. Understanding and value motives, and protective and esteem motives, were significantly related as in Study 1. Esteem and understanding motives also were significantly related. Also, caregiver satisfaction was significantly positively related to value, esteem, and protective motives. No further inter-scale coefficients were significantly related.

Initial and Follow-Up Comparisons on Self-Reported Inventory Scores. A series of t-tests for paired samples were performed on mean scale scores at the initial and follow-up sessions. There was no significant difference between initial and 14 week follow-up on the volunteer motives, caregiver experiences, or religiosity. In fact, the only significant difference was in social desirability, with participants reporting less of a need for social approval from the first test session, $M = 20.4$ (SD = 3.8), to the last test session, $M = 14.8$ (SD = 4.2), $t (20) = 4.26, p < .001$.

Discussion

This second study supports Study 1, yet expands those results. Consistent with that study, students reported several volunteer motives related to each other: values with understanding, and protective with esteem. These findings replicate across different student samples, at different institutions, serving in different sites. Further, Study 2 showed that a sense of satisfaction as a care provided was positively related to value and understanding, as well as esteem, motives for service. It seems that a positive, "good feeling" one gets from providing volunteer care to others reflects the person's prosocial values, offers a sense of understanding of those receiving the care, and relieves any negative feelings from volunteering. These relations are independent of

TABLE 2. Mean Scores, Coefficient Alpha, and Zero-Order Correlates Between Self-Reported Psychometric Inventories in Study 2

MEASURE	M	(1)	(2)	(3)	(4)	(5)	(6)	(7)	(8)	(9)	(10)	(11)
VOLUNTEER FUNCTIONING MOTIVES:												
(1) social	10.14	[.71]										
(2) values	28.52	-.21	[.86]									
(3) career	21.86	.26	.09	[.87]								
(4) understanding	27.05	.33	.44*	.29	[.83]							
(5) esteem	17.29	.28	.11	-.03	.47*	[.83]						
(6) protective	15.81	.22	.33	.15	.28	.49*	[.68]					
CAREGIVER EXPERIENCE:												
(7) satisfaction	27.10	.11	.57*	-.06	.61	.65*	.54*	[.87]				
(8) stress	11.21	-.21	.12	-.05	.05	.05	.11	.04	[.85]			
RELIGIOSITY:												
(9) external	33.84	.16	.00	.11	.25	.10	.45	.02	.28	[.69]		
(10) internal	27.90	.01	.20	-.27	.15	.26	-.23	.39	.09	-.31	[.73]	
SOCIAL DESIRABILITY:												
(11)	19.13	.10	-.37	.79*	-.08	-.14	-.05	-.38	.14	-.18	-.44	[.86]

$n = 21$ *$p < .05$

Note: Value in brackets is coefficient alpha.

social desirability, and do not relate with a person's sense of religious preference. Taken together with the first study, it seems that community-service, even those involved because of mandatory course requirements and over long periods of time, has a positive, constructive impact on young adult students.

STUDY 3

This study focused on adults who were trained as professional caregivers: psychologists. Unlike the first two studies, these were more mature adults who received doctoral training (typically in clinical courses) in psychology to provide service to others. All respondents were working professionals, and this survey assessed the role of their education on their current community-service experiences. Because it was exploratory in nature, no *a priori* hypotheses were made, except that we thought that volunteerism rates would be high among this select sample of professionals.

Method

Participants. There were a total of 188 individuals from a medium-size, private, midwestern university who graduated from psychology doctoral programs that were eligible for inclusion into this study because accurate, current mailing addresses were available from departmental files (representing 91.3% of the graduates from 1980 to 1996). From this sample, 140 were clinical doctoral graduates and 48 were experimental or industrial-organizational (non-clinical) doctoral graduates.

A total of 42 graduates (34 clinical, 8 non-clinical) participated in the present mailed survey, representing a sample of 22.3% of all graduates. In terms of self-reported demographic items, these 22 men and 20 women reported that they were entering middle age (*M* age = 38.1 years old, *SD* = 5.8), mostly white (88.1% Caucasian, 4.8% African-American, 2.4 % Asian-American, and 4.8% undeclared), and married (76.2% married, 16.7% single, 7.1% divorced/separated). Most respondents also indicated that they were employed full-time (87.7%) at private affiliations or businesses (54.8%) making a middle-class income (*M* = $61,071; *SD* = $10,333).

In terms of community volunteerism and educational training, participants reported that they offer on average 1.8 days per week to community volunteer service, and have performed this service for the past 34.8 months. During this time they held the same type of service role, with a mean of 1.5 different roles assumed. In terms of educational training impacting on their sense of community service, participants reported that while in graduate school their field exposures had a greater impact (*M* = 4.1; *SD* = 0.9) than their classroom experiences (*M* = 3.3; *SD* = 0.8) in shaping their future sense of community service, t (40) = $-.369, p < .001$.

Psychometric Measures and Procedures. All graduates were mailed a brief description of the purpose of this survey to examine community service experiences, and were asked to complete a set of items and scales which could be returned to the first author in addressed, postage paid envelopes. The first author was not familiar with these individuals since they had graduated before the start of his faculty position. Consent to participate was determined by returning the completed set of measures. Demographic items included age, gender, marital status, ethnic identity, current employment status and income, present community volunteerism experiences, and aspects of their doctoral education experiences.

Also, graduates were asked to complete the VFI and SD measures discussed above, as well as Carver and Schier's (1995) revised 12-items, 4-point rating scale *Life Orientation Test* (LOT), a well used and very reliable and valid measure of optimism toward one's life. Participants also completed Wolford's (1996) new 12-item, 8-point rating scale *Empowerment* inventory which assessed a person's sense of competence and efficacy to make a differences in their community, family, and personal life. This unpublished scale asks respondents to indicate whether they have a sense of personal power, enthusiasm for making change, general sense of well-being, and hope for positive future outcomes with each of these three target domains. The four items per target domain are summed for an empowerment score for community, family and personal life. Little information on the measures reliability and validity were available at the present time, so the current study appears to be the first published paper reporting use of this measure. Coefficient alphas for these three target empowerment domains, along with the others scales used in Study 3, are found in Table 3 below.

Results

The small number of clinical and non-clinical respondents to this survey prohibited comparisons between these groups on demographic and self-reported measures. Visual inspection of their mean scores and frequencies, however, suggested no large difference on most demographic items and the psychometric measures used in this study. Therefore, no comparisons between these groups was conducted, and all further analyses were based on the total sample.

Correlates Between Self-Reported Inventory Scores. Table 3 presents the mean score, coefficient alpha, and inter-scale correlates among measures

TABLE 3. Mean Scores, Coefficient Alpha, and Zero-Order Correlates Between Self-Reported Psychometric Inventories in Study 3

MEASURE	M	(1)	(2)	(3)	(4)	(5)	(6)	(7)	(8)	(9)	(10)	(11)
VOLUNTEER FUNCTIONING MOTIVES:												
(1) social	15.38	[.80]										
(2) values	27.51	.19	[.73]									
(3) career	12.83	.03	-.29	[.84]								
(4) understanding	20.05	.48*	.57*	.08	[.80]							
(5) esteem	16.83	.45*	.17	.26	.52*	[.77]						
(6) protective	10.19	.22	.27	.08	.38*	.48*	[.68]					
OPTIMISM:												
(7)	17.95	-.02	.46*	.01	.38*	.19	-.01	[.82]				
EMPOWERMENT:												
(8) community	21.28	.09	.42*	.04	.19	-.06	-.14	.24	[.76]			
(9) family	25.74	-.14	.18	.06	-.07	-.05	.05	.39*	.38*	[.78]		
(10) personal	27.00	.16	.35*	.06	.29	.00	-.10	.56*	.40*	.68*	[.66]	
SOCIAL DESIRABILITY:												
(11)	20.05	.13	-.04	-.01	.17	.09	.12	.11	.25	-.11	.09	[.80]

$n = 42$ $p < .05$

Note: Value in brackets is coefficient alpha.

used in this study. As noted from the table, social desirability was not significantly related with any of these self-reported measures. Examining the table it appears that volunteer motives of values and understanding were the highest reported motives for community service. An understanding motive was significantly positively related to social, value, esteem, and protective motives, and an esteem motive was significantly positively related to social and protective motives.

In addition, the volunteer motive of values was significantly positively related to personal optimism and a sense of empowerment with both one's community and personal life. The motive of understanding also was significantly positively related to personal optimism. Also, personal optimism was significantly positively related to family and personal empowerment. All three target areas of empowerment were significantly positively interrelated with each other.

Discussion

It is interesting that among the respondents to this study (both clinical and non-clinical professional psychologists) active involvement in community service was reported. Responses to survey measures were not independent of social desirability, although the number of respondents were low suggesting the potential for a biased sample of participants in this study. Nevertheless, respondents indicated a sense of optimism in their life and felt a sense of community commitment toward helping others. Future studies are needed to expand the implications of these results, but the data do suggest that professional psychologists may be involved in their local community as volunteers.

GENERAL CONCLUSION

The present set of studies were very exploratory: no major hypotheses on community service were proposed or evaluated. Still, the results seem striking when compared across samples, settings, and situations. In all three studies some volunteer motives (independent of social desirability) were significantly positively related, as predicted by Clary et al. (1992). Values and understanding were significantly related. These motives were classified as "selfless" motives (Snyder, 1993), reflecting that people may become involved in helping others in order to fulfill their civic or social responsibilities. Furthermore, the motives of protective and esteem were significantly related, identified as "selfish" motives (Snyder, 1993), where community service originates from a personal need to help others. Taken together, these results indicate that BOTH personal and other-oriented motives influence volunteerism.

These results also indicate that the value motives were negatively related to a desire not to control the "help-ees," but related to caregiving satisfaction, personal life optimism, and empowerment over one's community and personal life. The understanding motive also was positively related to optimism. These results indicate that selfless motives for volunteering are associated with positive, socially desirable personal factors. Both esteem and protective motives were negatively related to being decisive and positively related to caregiver satisfaction. It seems based on these results that volunteer selfish motives still give a person a feeling of satisfaction in helping others.

Of course, further research is needed. The small number of participants in each of these studies may limit the generalizability of the present results. Similar scales, other than the VFI and SD, were not used across all three studies. An understanding of the theoretical bases for volunteerism also was not proposed nor evaluated in any of these three studies. Nevertheless, we believe that the present set of projects do provide some additional knowledge about volunteerism in America. The need for involvement in social ills is apparent, especially as our society enters a new century with limited resources but expanding civic problems. Community service may be one way we can make-a-difference in the lives of others.

REFERENCES

Allport, G.W., & Rosa, J. M. (1967). Personal religious orientation and prejudice. *Journal of Personality and Social Psychology, 5*, 423-443.

Bishop, P.D., Chertok, F., & Jason, L.A. (1997). Measuring sense of community: Beyond local boundaries. *Journal of Primary Prevention, 18*, 193-212.

Bishop, P.D., Jason, L.A., Ferrari, J.R., & Shu, C.F. (in press). A survival analysis of communal-living, self-help, addiction recovery participants. *American Journal of Community Psychology*.

Burger, J.M., & Cooper, H.M. (1979). The desirability of control. Motivation and Emotion, *3*, 381-393.

Clary, E.G., Snyder, M., & Ridge, R. (1992). Volunteers' motivations: A functional strategy for the recruitment, placement, and retention of volunteers. *Non-Profit Management and Leadership, 2*, 333-350.

Clary, E.G., Snyder, M., & Stukas, A. (1996). *Service-learning and psychology: Lessons from the psychology of volunteers' motivations.* Unpublished manuscript, College of Saint Catherine and University of Minnesota.

Crowne, D.P., & Marlowe, D. (1960). A new scale of social desirability independent of psychopathology. *Journal of Consulting Psychology, 24*, 349-354.

Donahue, M.J. (1985). Intrinsic and extrinsic religiousness: Review and meta-analysis. *Journal of Personality and Social Psychology, 48*, 400-419.

Ferrari, J.R., Billows, W., Jason, L.A., & Grill, G.J. (1997). Matching the needs of the homeless with those of the disabled: Empowerment through care-giving. *Journal of Prevention & Intervention in the Community, 15*, 83-92.

Ferrari, J.R., & Geller, E.S. (1994). Developing future care-givers by integrating research and community service. *The Community Psychologist, 27,* 12-13.

Ferrari, J.R., & Jason, L.A. (1997a). Integrating research and community service: Incorporating research skills into service learning experiences. *College Student Journal, 30,* 444-451.

Ferrari, J.R., & Jason, L.A. (1997b). Caring for people with Chronic Fatigue Syndrome: Perceived stress versus satisfaction. *Rehabilitation Counseling Bulletin, 40,* 240-251.

Ferrari, J.R., Jason, L.A., & Salina, D. (1995). Pastoral care and AIDS: Assessing the stress and satisfaction from caring for persons with AIDS. *Pastoral Psychology, 44,* 99-110.

Ferrari, J.R., McCown, W., & Pantano, J. (1993). Experiencing satisfaction and stress as an AIDS care-provider: "The (AIDS) Caregivers" Scale. *Evaluation and the Health Professions, 16,* 295-310.

Harrison, C.H. (1987). Student service: The New Carnegie Unit (ISBN-0-931050-30-8). *The Carnegie Foundation for the Advancement of Teaching,* Princeton, NJ.

Independent Sector (1990). Volunteering and giving among American teenagers 14 to 17 years of age: *Finding from a Nation Survey Independent Sector,* Washington, DC.

Kirby, K. (1989). Community Service and Civic Education sponsoring agency: Washington DC: *Office of Educational Research and Improvement.*

Kirkpatrick, L.A., & Hood, R.W. (1990). Intrinsic-extrinsic religious orientation: The boon and bane of contemporary psychology of religion. *Journal for the Scientific Study of Religion, 29,* 442-462.

Moore, C.W., & Allen, J.P. (1996). The facts of volunteering on the young volunteer. *The Journal of Primary Prevention, 17,* 231-258.

Newmann, F.A., & Rutter, R.A. (1983). The effects of high school community service programs on students' social development: Final Report. *Wisconsin Center for Educational Research,* 107 pages.

Omoto, A.M., & Snyder, M. (1990). Basic research in action: Volunteerism and society's response to AIDS. *Personality and Social Psychology Bulletin, 16,* 152-165.

Scheier, M.F., Carver, C.S., & Bridges, M.W. (1994). Distinguishing optimism from neuroticism (and Trait Anxiety, Self Mastery, and Self Esteem): A Re-evaluation of the Life Orientation Test. *Journal of Personality and Social Psychology, 67,* 1063-1078.

Snyder, M. (1993). Basic research and practical problems: The promise of a "functional" personality and social psychology. *Personality and Social Psychology Bulletin, 19,* 251-264.

Wolford, G.A. (1996). *The use asset planning groups in the community.* Unpublished manuscript, Greenwich University, Cotter, AR.

Youth Service America (1988). The time is right: A report of the Youth Service America and Brown University Youth Service Leadership Conference. Paper presented at Providence, RI, Feb. 25-26.

Medical Student Motivations to Volunteer: Gender Differences and Comparisons to Other Volunteers

Carrie L. Switzer
Galen E. Switzer
Arthur A. Stukas
Carol E. Baker

University of Pittsburgh

SUMMARY. This investigation examined medical students' motivations for participating in a volunteer community-based program for pregnant women provided primarily to traditionally underserved groups. Demographic, psychosocial, and motivational characteristics of 40 students participating in the Maternal Care Program were assessed with a self-report instrument. Medical students' motivations to participate (assessed in 6 volunteer motive categories) were higher in all categories than those found in previous studies of active adult volunteers, and university students. The rank-ordering of the importance of the motive categories also differed for medical students compared to the other groups. Finally, important differences in both the strength and the rank-ordering of motivations was found for male and female medical students. These group and gender differences are discussed in terms of their theoretical importance, as well as their practical implications for how medical schools might recruit students, encourage volunteerism, and foster more positive relationships with underserved communities. *[Article copies available for a fee from The Haworth Document Delivery Service: 1-800-342-9678. E-mail address: getinfo@haworthpressinc.com]*

Address correspondence to: Carrie L. Switzer, University of Pittsburgh, G-33 Cathedral of Learning, Pittsburgh, PA 15260 (E-mail: clsst35@vms.cis.pitt.edu).

[Haworth co-indexing entry note]: "Medical Student Motivations to Volunteer: Gender Differences and Comparisons to Other Volunteers." Switzer, Carrie L. et al. Co-published simultaneously in *Journal of Prevention & Intervention in the Community* (The Haworth Press, Inc.) Vol. 18, No. 1/2, 1999, pp. 53-64; and: *Educating Students to Make-a-Difference: Community-Based Service Learning* (ed: Joseph R. Ferrari, and Judith G. Chapman) The Haworth Press, Inc., 1999, pp. 53-64. Single or multiple copies of this article are available for a fee from The Haworth Document Delivery Service [1-800-342-9678, 9:00 a.m. - 5:00 p.m. (EST). E-mail address: getinfo@haworthpressinc.com].

With the implementation of managed care, the medical establishment has been faced with the challenge of a growing demand for primary care physicians who will provide equal access to care for traditionally underserved populations (i.e., the uninsured and urban and rural poor). An approach used by some medical schools to affect positive student attitudes about the medically underserved and the choice of a primary care specialty is through direct experience with these populations (Tippets & Westpheling, 1996; Verby, Newell, Andresen, & Swentko, 1991). One of the best ways for medical students to gain exposure to the medically underserved has been through *volunteering* at: (a) inner-city free clinics (Hamilton, 1993); (b) community AIDS programs (Cohen & Cohen, 1991); and, (c) clinics and outreach programs for the homeless (Collins, 1995). Although it has not yet been empirically verified, it is anticipated that positive volunteer experiences may enhance students' willingness to work in a primary care capacity and lead to more positive attitudes about the medically underserved. It would therefore, be important for medical schools to effectively recruit and retain students for volunteer programs. Since motivations play an essential role in this process, it is critical to study the motivations medical students have to volunteer, if there are gender differences in motivation, and if medical student motivations differ from those of other groups.

In the present study we examined a volunteer program that allowed medical students the opportunity to gain both primary care clinical experience and exposure to a medically underserved population. The specific aims of the study were to: (a) describe the type of students who volunteered for a maternal care program; (b) examine whether medical students compared to other groups have different motives for volunteering; and, (c) examine whether there were gender differences in medical students' motivations to volunteer. We expected that more female than male medical students would volunteer for this program given that the volunteer experience examined here centers around helping women through the prenatal care and birth process. Because this volunteer experience was one of the few ways the medical students could gain experience with actual patients in their first year of school we suspected that they might be more motivated to volunteer to gain knowledge or for reasons related to their careers as compared to other volunteers. Finally, among medical students, we expected females more often than males to report motives related to a desire to help others because they may be more socialized to be nurturing and caring (Eagly & Crowley, 1986).

MOTIVATION AND MEDICAL STUDENT VOLUNTEERISM

Functional Approach to Volunteer Motivation

In general, functional theorists have sought to understand how individuals' psychological and social needs, goals, plans, and motives are satisfied through their beliefs and behaviors. It is theorized that different people may engage in similar behaviors in order to satisfy very different psychological functions (Katz, 1960; Smith, Bruner, & White, 1956).

Clary, Snyder, and their colleagues have applied the basic concepts of the functionalist approach to volunteer behavior (Clary & Snyder, 1991; Clary, Snyder, & Ridge, 1992; Clary, Snyder, & Stukas, 1996). Using this framework they suggest that people volunteer for a variety of personal and social reasons and that identical volunteer activities may fulfill different goals for different people. These personal and social reasons for volunteering are captured in six broad volunteer motivations that comprise the Volunteer Functions Inventory (VFI). The motivations include: (a) *Understanding*–To gain knowledge and perspective and to practice skills, (b) *Values*–To express concern for those in need, (c) *Enhancement*–To strive for personal growth and self-esteem, (d) *Career*–To gain career related benefits like experience to put on a resume, (e) *Social*–To participate in an activity that is viewed favorably by close others or to spend time with friends, and (f) *Protective*–To alleviate negative feelings like guilt over being more fortunate than others. The six subscales of the VFI have been found to have internal consistency and temporal stability among divergent groups of people (Clary, Snyder, Ridge, Copeland, Stukas, Haugen, & Miene, in press).

Volunteer Motivation and Medical Students

As noted previously, volunteering exposes medical students to primary care settings and underserved populations and provides clinical experience that is sometimes difficult to incorporate into the first two years of medical school. The motivations medical students have for volunteering have been previously unexplored and their examination is important for a number of reasons. First, recruiting techniques may be more effective if they match a person's motives for volunteering (Clary et al., in press). Second, people may be more effective volunteers and more satisfied with their efforts if their volunteer opportunities match their personal motives to help (Clary & Snyder, 1991; Clary et al., in press). Third, volunteers with certain motives (e.g., Values) are more likely than those reporting other motives to complete their service tenure (Clary & Miller, 1986; Clary & Orenstein, 1991). Finally, volunteers whose benefits from volunteering match their motives to volunteer are more likely to perceive themselves as volunteering in the future (Clary et al., in press). Therefore, the motivations medical students have to volunteer may be linked to the effectiveness with which they are recruited for a specific program, their effectiveness and satisfaction with volunteering, whether or not they will complete a volunteer program, and whether they will continue to volunteer in the future.

Motivations to volunteer have been studied in a variety of groups including active adult volunteers, university students, and elderly volunteers (Clary et al., in press). An interesting question not yet examined is how medical student motivations compare to those of other groups. Therefore, a second goal of this paper is to examine the similarities and differences among the motivations of medical student volunteers from the Maternal Care Program, active adult volunteers, and undergraduate university students.

GENDER DIFFERENCES IN VOLUNTEERING

Social Role Theory of Helping

In addition to the importance of studying an individual's motivation to volunteer, there are indications that gender plays an essential role in helping behavior. For example, Eagly and Crowley's (1986) social role theory suggests that helping behaviors are differentiated by gender. Socialization propels males and females in different helping trajectories that are consistent with their sex roles. In general, females are raised to be nurturing and caring and are therefore more likely to show empathy for someone and to provide emotional support. Society expects women to be self-sacrificing and to help others attain their goals. As a result, women are more likely to feel comfortable in helping situations that are more intimate and long-term.

Men are socialized in ways that promote heroic and chivalrous helping. Men are expected to help in dangerous situations and especially if strangers are in need of assistance. Helping in risky situations is strengthened for men if there are other people observing the helping act. Therefore, males may feel more comfortable in short-term helping situations that involve a stranger, have an audience, and involve some risk (Eagly & Crowley, 1986). Although social role theory refers to helping *behaviors,* we suspect that such socialization may also play a role in an individual's motivation to help.

Gender Differences in Medical Student Motivations

Numerous studies have found gender differences in the psychosocial characteristics of medical students and physicians. According to Grant, Genero, Nurius, Moore, and Brown (1986), female medical students tend to be more humanitarian than male students. Fourth-year female medical students were found to be generally less cynical about health care issues than their male counterparts. In addition, first and fourth-year female students felt a greater sense of personal responsibility for providing medical care and had more positive attitudes about indigent populations than did male students (Crandall, Volk, & Loemker, 1993). A study of practicing physicians found females to be more liberal, egalitarian, and sensitive than male physicians (Heins, Hendricks, Martindale, Smock, Stein, & Jacobs, 1979).

In the present study we will use the social role theory of gender differences in helping as a guide for explaining gender differences in the motives medical students have for volunteering. Based on the evidence from studies within the medical profession we expect that female medical students will rate expressing concern for others (Values) as a more important motive for volunteerism than male medical students. We will use the functional approach to volunteer motivations as a framework to evaluate differences in medical students', active adult volunteers', and undergraduate students' motivations to volunteer. Specifically, since people volunteer for a variety of personal and social reasons, we expect medical students to be more motivated to volunteer to gain understanding and for career benefits than other volunteers.

METHOD

Site and Study Participants

The current study was conducted in conjunction with the Maternal Care Program at a Midwestern medical school. This voluntary program pairs first and second year medical students with free clinic/low income or private practice/middle income, pregnant women. The medical students follow the women through their pregnancy by going to prenatal appointments, offering support and information, and attending the birth. For many of the students this is one of the few opportunities to gain clinical experience during the first two years of medical school as well as work with an underserved population.

Forty of 60 medical students (67%) who signed up for the Maternal Care Program participated in our study. The medical students who were nonparticipants in the study either chose not to participate, were not assigned a mother with whom to volunteer due to a shortage of mothers, or had a mother who dropped out of the program shortly after signing up. The majority of medical students in our sample were in their first year of medical school (90%), Caucasian (93%), and female (63%) with an average age of 23.85 years old (SD = 3.2). The top specialty choices were: (a) Family Medicine, (b) Obstetrics-Gynecology, and (c) Internal Medicine. The majority of students described themselves as being people who at least sometimes volunteer to help others (98%) and who would be disappointed in themselves if they did not help (93%). Sixty percent of the students indicated they were at least somewhat committed to working with underserved populations and planned to provide at least part-time volunteer service in a medically underserved area. Thirty-five percent of the students planned to provide paid service to an underserved population. The majority of students (92%) had volunteered at another organization prior to their involvement with the Maternal Care Program.

Procedure

Self-report questionnaires were administered to students at the beginning of their volunteer experience in the Fall, 1996, by the coordinator of the Maternal Care Program. In the Spring and Summer, 1997, follow-up questionnaires were administered to students at the conclusion of their volunteer experience; after the mother with whom they volunteered gave birth. The medical students were assured that their responses were confidential and that no one at their school would have access to their questionnaires. In addition to collecting demographic information, students' motivations for volunteering were assessed using the Volunteer Functions Inventory (Clary et al., in press).

Measures

Motivation. Medical students' motivations for volunteering were assessed using the *Volunteer Functions Inventory* (VFI), developed by Clary, Snyder, and their colleagues. The VFI is a 30 item scale consisting of six subscales with each subscale containing five items. Students were asked to indicate "how important each of the following reasons for volunteering were for them" using a response scale anchored by 1 (not at all important/ accurate) and 7 (extremely important/accurate). Scale scores were obtained by averaging scores on the five items. Individuals' scores on each scale could range from 1.0 to 7.0; the higher the score, the greater the importance of that specific motivation. The following are the six subscales for the VFI:

  a. *Values*–To express concern for those in need, for example, "I am concerned about those less fortunate than myself," (M = 5.91,SD = 0.79) the Cronbach alpha for the current sample = 0.87; previous alpha [Clary et al., in press] = 0.80,
  b. *Understanding*To gain knowledge and to practice skills, for example, "Volunteering lets me learn through direct "hands on" experience," (M = 5.92, SD = 0.77) current alpha = 0.82; previous alpha = 0.81,
  c. *Enhancement*–To strive for personal growth and self-esteem, for example, "Volunteering makes me feel needed," (M = 4.49, SD = 1.22) current alpha = 0.84; previous alpha = 0.84,

d. *Protective*–To alleviate negative feelings like guilt over being more fortunate than others, for example, "No matter how bad I've been feeling, volunteering helps me to forget about it," (M = 3.35, SD = 1.25) current alpha = 0.86; previous alpha = 0.81,

e. *Social*–To participate in an activity that is viewed favorably by those close to the volunteer or to spend time with friends, for example, "Others with whom I am close place a high value on community service," (M = 3.41, SD = 1.20) current alpha = 0.86; previous alpha = 0.83, and

f. *Career*–To gain career related benefits, for example, "Volunteering allows me to explore different career options," (M = 4.57, SD = 1.15) current alpha = 0.78; previous alpha = 0.89.

RESULTS

VFI Differences Between Medical Students, Adult Volunteers, and Undergraduates

A central research question of this study was whether or not medical students' motivations to volunteer as assessed by the Volunteer Functions Inventory (VFI) differed from other groups. Data for two comparison groups were obtained from Clary et al. (in press). The first comparison group was active adult volunteers (*N* = 467) from 5 organizations in a metropolitan area. The volunteer programs ranged from disaster relief and help for the physically handicapped, to public health services. The average age for the adult volunteers was 40.9 years (*SD* = 13.38). The second comparison group was undergraduate introductory psychology students attending the same university (*N* = 535). Sixty percent of the sample had previous volunteer experience. The average age for the undergraduates was 21.25 years (*SD* = 4.99). Our sample of medical students (*N* = 40) were current volunteers in the Maternal Care Program. Ninety-two percent of the medical students reported previous volunteer experience and their average age was 23.85 years (*SD* = 3.20).

As indicated in Table 1, for both the adult volunteers and university students ordering of the motivation subscales was identical, with Values being the most important motive followed by Understanding and Enhancement. However, for the medical students, Understanding and Values resulted in the highest ranks, followed by Career. Interestingly, the medical students had higher average scores on all of the motivation subscales compared to the adult volunteers. The medical students also had higher average scores on all of the subscales with the exception of Enhancement when compared to the university students.

VFI Gender Differences Between Medical Students

It was predicted that, given the well-documented differences in psycho-social characteristics of male and female medical students and physicians, there would be gender differences in the importance of volunteer motivations. As shown in Table 2, male and female medical students do rate the subscales of the Volunteer Functions Inventory differently. Males were more motivated to volunteer to gain knowledge and practice skills (Understanding); express concern for others (Values), and receive career related benefits (Career). Female medical students were more motivated to volunteer by the need to express concern for others (Values), to gain knowledge and practice skills (Understanding), and for personal growth and self-esteem (Enhancement).

The differences in the VFI motivation subscale means were compared using t-tests. Female medical students (M = 6.08, SD = .71) rated Values

TABLE 1. VFI Ranking for Medical Students, Active Adult Volunteers*, and University Students*

Motivation	Medical Students M (SD) N = 40	Rank	Active Adult Volunteers* M (SD) N = 467	Rank	University Students* M (SD) N = 535	Rank
Understanding	5.92 (.77)	1	4.91 (1.32)	2	5.13 (1.20)	2
Values	5.91 (.79)	2	5.82 (1.00)	1	5.37 (1.17)	1
Career	4.57 (1.15)	3	2.74 (1.64)	4	4.54 (1.50)	4
Enhancement	4.49 (1.22)	4	4.27 (1.43)	3	4.64 (1.36)	3
Social	3.41 (1.20)	5	2.59 (1.30)	6	2.95 (1.28)	6
Protective	3.35 (1.25)	6	2.61 (1.37)	5	3.25 (1.36)	5

*Data for Active Adult Volunteers and University Students are taken from Clary et al. (in press).

TABLE 2. VFI Ranking for Male and Female Medical Students

Motivation	Females M (SD) n = 25	Rank	Males M (SD) n = 15	Rank
Values	6.08 (.71)	1	5.62 (.86)**	2
Understanding	6.00 (.79)	2	5.79 (.72)	1
Enhancement	4.69 (1.29)	3	4.16 (1.06)*	4
Career	4.66 (1.17)	4	4.44 (1.15)	3
Protective	3.50 (1.30)	5	3.09 (1.17)	6
Social	3.23 (1.26)	6	3.70 (1.08)	5

*p < .10 ** p < .05.

motives significantly higher than male medical students ($M = 5.62$, $SD = .86$), $t(25.30) = 1.75$, $p < .05$. Female medical students ($M = 4.69$, $SD = 1.29$) also rated Enhancement motives significantly higher than male medical students ($M = 4.16$, $SD = 1.06$), $t(34.28) = 1.41$, $p < .08$. Because the small sample decreases our power to detect differences between groups we have also discussed differences whose magnitude produces p values of .10 and below. Although the differences did not reach statistical significance, with the exception of the Social subscale, females tended to be higher on all of the motivation subscales than were males.

An important note is that the importance of specific motivations to volunteer differ for male and female medical students. Female medical students rate the motivation subscales in the same order of importance as the two comparison groups discussed in the previous section. The difference in the order of the motivation subscales for medical students compared to active adult volunteers and university students is due solely to the importance that *male* medical students place on the motives to volunteer.

DISCUSSION

Motivational Differences Between Groups

Our investigation of medical student motives for volunteering focused on a group of students participating in a Maternal Care Program. A central research question in our study was whether or not these students' motivations for volunteering differed from other groups. The two groups we compared to the medical students were: (a) active adult volunteers, and (b) undergraduate university students. Our examination showed that one of the most important motivations for all three groups was to express their concern for others (Values). Acquiring knowledge and practicing new skills (Understanding) was also important for the three groups. However, medical students appeared to be more motivated by the opportunity to gain experience that would help them in their profession (Career) when compared to the adult volunteers and to a lesser degree when compared to the university students. In contrast, the adult volunteers and university students were more motivated by personal development and increased self-esteem (Enhancement) through volunteering than the medical students. With the exception of the Enhancement subscale for university students, the medical students rated all of the motivation subscales higher than the comparison groups. This seems to indicate that medical students are highly motivated volunteers even when compared to current adult volunteers.

There are several implications medical schools can draw from these findings that would be useful in recruiting and retaining student volunteers. Clary et al. (in press) found that university students judged recruitment ads for volunteer programs to be more persuasive if the ads matched their personal motives for volunteering. Medical schools may find the recruitment of medical students for volunteer programs more effective if they emphasize aspects of their programs that allow students to learn new information and practice clinical skills they can later use as physicians. Satisfaction with and retention in volunteer programs has also been linked to the compatibility of individuals' motives for volunteering and the benefits they received from the experience (Clary et al., in press). Therefore, medical schools may want to emphasize volunteer programs that allow students the opportunity to express concern for others and allow for personal growth.

Gender Differences in Medical Student Motivation

Social role theory suggests that males and females are socialized to help in different ways (Eagly & Crowley, 1986). Therefore, we predicted gender differences in motivations for volunteering among medical students, specifically on the Values motivation. As expected, there were differences in the importance males and females gave to the various motives for volunteering. Female medical students rated expressing concern for others (Values) and striving for personal growth and self-esteem (Enhancement) significantly higher than male medical students. Both males and females rated gaining knowledge and practicing skills (Understanding) as an important motivation to volunteer. Even though it did not reach statistical significance, male medical students placed more importance on volunteering to gain knowledge and skills that would help them in their profession (Career) than female medical students. According to social role theory, females are socialized to be nurturing, caring, and self-sacrificing when providing help (Eagly & Crowley, 1986). Therefore, its not surprising that important motivations for female medical students to volunteer would be expressing concern for others and personal growth.

Even thought the differences between male and female medical students' motivations were significantly different for only two of the subscales (e.g., Values and Enhancement), female medical students rated all the motivations higher than males with the exception of the Social subscale. This seems to indicate that even though male medical students are highly motivated, female medical students may be slightly more motivated to volunteer. These gender differences concur with findings from a national survey of adults conducted for Independent Sector where females also rated the motivations to volunteer higher than males (Clary et al., 1996).

Given that medical students have demonstrated gender differences in the motives for volunteering they find the most important, medical schools may want to offer a variety of volunteer opportunities to reach the widest number of students. For instance, programs that emphasize an expression of concern for others and personal growth for the volunteer may fulfill more of the needs of female medical students. Male medical students may be more satisfied with technical programs that emphasize skill development.

Two potential limitations for this study should be noted. First, the data reported are from self-report questionnaires and even though the medical students were assured of their anonymity some may have responded in ways they felt were socially or politically desirable. Second, our sample is relatively small and contains more Caucasian and female students than the national average for the 1996-1997 medical student body. Our sample is 93% Caucasian and during the 1996-1997 school year 68% of the graduates from medical schools were Caucasian. Our sample is 63% female and during the 1996-1997 school year 42% of students enrolled in medical schools were female (Association of American Medical Colleges, 1997). Therefore, a larger sample that is closer to the gender and racial composition of the national medical student body is an important next step in the process.

This project focused on examining differences between medical students' motives for volunteering and the motives prevalent in other volunteer groups, and on gender differences in motives within the medical student sample. The next critical step should be to longitudinally assess both motivations and psychosocial and behavioral outcomes as medical students participate in volunteer programs to determine if type and intensity of motivation is related to positive outcomes for students.

REFERENCES

Association of American Medical Colleges. (1997, November). *Fall enrollment questionnaire and reported graduates report, AAMC section for student services.* Washington, DC: Author.

Clary, E. G., & Miller, J. (1986). Socialization and situational influences on sustained altruism. *Child Development, 57,* 1358-1369.

Clary, E. G., & Orenstein, L. (1991). The amount and effectiveness of help: The relationship of motives and abilities to helping behavior. *Personality and Social Psychology Bulletin, 17,* 58-64.

Clary, E. G., & Snyder, M. (1991). A functional analysis of altruism and prosocial behavior: The case of volunteerism. *Review of Personality and Social Psychology, 12,* 119-148.

Clary, E. G., Snyder, M., & Ridge, R. D. (1992). Volunteers' motivations: A functional strategy for the recruitment, placement, and retention of volunteers. *Nonprofit Management & Leadership, 2,* 333-350.

Clary, E. G., Snyder, M., Ridge, R. D., Copeland, J., Stukas, A. A., Haugen, J., & Miene, P. (in press). Understanding and assessing the motivations of volunteers: A functional approach. *Journal of Personality and Social Psychology.*

Clary, E. G., Snyder, M., & Stukas, A. A. (1996). Volunteers' motivations: Findings from a national survey. *Nonprofit and Voluntary Sector Quarterly, 25*(4), 485-505.

Cohen, M. A. A., & Cohen, S. C. (1991). AIDS education and a volunteer training program for medical students. *Psychosomatics, 32*(2), 187-190.

Collins, A. C. (1995). The Hahnemann Homeless Clinics Project: Taking health care to the streets and shelters. *Journal of the American Medical Association, 273*(5), 433.

Crandall, S. J. S., Volk, R. J., & Loemker, V. (1993). Medical students' attitudes toward providing care for the underserved: Are we training socially responsible physicians? *Journal of the American Medical Association, 269*(19), 2519-2523.

Eagly, A., & Crowley, M. (1986). Gender and helping behavior: A meta-analytic review of the social psychological literature. *Psychological Bulletin, 100*, 283-308.

Grant, L., Genero, N., Nurius, P., Moore, W. E., & Brown, D. R. (1986). Gender and time variations in medical students' value development. *Sex Roles, 15*, 95-108.

Hamilton, S. (1993). Milwaukee's medical students rise to meet Milwaukee's need. *Wisconsin Medical Journal, 92*(10), 575-578.

Heins, M., Hendricks, J., Martindale, L., Smock, S., Stein, M., & Jacobs, J. (1979). Attitudes of women and men physicians. *American Journal of Public Health, 69*, 1132-1139.

Katz, D. (1960). The functional approach to the study of attitudes. *Public Opinion Quarterly, 24*, 163-204.

Smith, M. B., Bruner, J., & White, R. (1956). *Opinions and personality.* New York: John Wiley.

Tippets, E., & Westpheling, K. (1996). The Health Promotion-Disease Prevention Project: Effect on medical students' attitudes toward practice in medically underserved areas. *Family Medicine, 28*(7), 467-471.

Verby, J. E., Newell, J. P., Andresen, S. A., & Swentko, W. M. (1991). Changing the medical school curriculum to improve patient access to primary care. *Journal of the American Medical Association, 266*(1), 110-113.

SERVICE AS LEARNING: STUDENT, FACULTY, AND COMMUNITY OUTCOMES

Clinical Application of the Service-Learning Model in Psychology: Evidence of Educational and Clinical Benefits

Roger N. Reeb
Julie A. Sammon
Nicole L. Isackson

University of Dayton

Address correspondence to: Roger N. Reeb, Department of Psychology, University of Dayton, 300 College Park, Dayton, OH 45469-1430 (E-mail: reeb@riker.stjoe.udayton.edu).

Spelling of the first author's surname was legally changed from "Rape" to "Reeb" on 4/28/95, and publications prior to that date are under the surname "Rape."

The authors acknowledge Kenneth J. Kuntz, Monalisa Mullins, and Nicholas J. Cardilino, University of Dayton, for their helpful suggestions in planning the project, as well as Ronald Reigelsperger, Montgomery County Juvenile Court of Ohio, for his ongoing support in project implementation.

This research was supported by grants from the Fund for Educational Development, University of Dayton.

[Haworth co-indexing entry note]: "Clinical Application of the Service-Learning Model in Psychology: Evidence of Educational and Clinical Benefits." Reeb, Roger N., Julie A. Sammon, and Nicole L. Isackson. Co-published simultaneously in *Journal of Prevention & Intervention in the Community* (The Haworth Press, Inc.) Vol. 18, No. 1/2, 1999, pp. 65-82; and: *Educating Students to Make-a-Difference: Community-Based Service Learning* (ed: Joseph R. Ferrari, and Judith G. Chapman) The Haworth Press, Inc., 1999, pp. 65-82. Single or multiple copies of this article are available for a fee from The Haworth Document Delivery Service [1-800-342-9678, 9:00 a.m. - 5:00 p.m. (EST). E-mail address: getinfo@haworthpressinc.com].

SUMMARY. Students in Abnormal Psychology who pursued a service-learning opportunity worked with troubled youth in the juvenile justice system. Consistent with an *a priori* hypothesis, results revealed the following pattern: (a) service-learning students and traditional students exhibited similar levels of academic performance early in the semester; and (b) as the semester progressed, and service-learning students became more involved in course-related service, they showed increasingly superior academic performance relative to traditional students. As hypothesized, service-learning students were more likely than traditional students to perceive themselves as: (a) achieving personal development in the area of social responsibility and (b) learning to apply course concepts to new situations. Preliminary evidence that the project made clinically significant contributions to the service agency is also presented. Innovations to be implemented in this ongoing project are discussed, and recommendations for research are noted. *[Article copies available for a fee from The Haworth Document Delivery Service: 1-800-342-9678. E-mail address: getinfo@haworthpressinc.com]*

The literature on the effects of service-learning on college students is limited. As noted by Miller (1994, p. 29), "Most of the literature that does exist is theoretical, philosophical, impressionistic, or anecdotal . . ." Nevertheless, there are some empirical findings to support the claim that, "when community service is combined with classroom instruction, the pedagogical advantages of each compensates for the shortcomings of the other" (Markus et al., 1993, p. 417). Research on the effects of service-learning have been published in the areas of psychology (Bringle & Kremer, 1993; McClusky-Fawcett & Green, 1992; Miller, 1994), political science (Markus et al., 1993), journalism (Cohen & Kinsey, 1994), and sociology (Kendrick, 1996).

The most commonly reported benefit of service-learning is that it promotes in students the development of social responsibility (e.g., Batchelder & Root, 1994; Kendrick, 1996; Markus et al., 1993; McClusky-Fawcett & Green, 1992). In general, the construct of social responsibility refers to a sense of citizenship obligations, awareness of social injustices, and a commitment to work toward social justice (Olney & Grande, 1995). To measure this construct, the Social Responsibility Inventory (Markus et al., 1993) is often used in this area of research.

In the service-learning literature, another outcome frequently examined is the students' mastery of course concepts. Empirical findings regarding this outcome are mixed, however. While some studies report that service-learning students learn course concepts at a higher level than do students who receive classroom instruction only (e.g., Markus et al., 1993), other studies do not find a significant group difference (e.g., Kendrick, 1996). In a thoughtful analysis of this problem, Miller (1994) has been able to pinpoint some methodological issues that may contribute to inconsistent findings.

First, in some of the earliest studies (e.g., Sugar & Livosky, 1988), it was reported that students who pursued an optional service experience obtained a higher final grade relative to students who did not pursue service; however, in some studies, the superior grade was a direct result of students receiving an extra-credit bonus for selecting the service option. Therefore, early studies were inconclusive regarding the effect of service-learning on students' mastery of course material. Recent studies have controlled for straightforward methodological problems, but other problems are evident, as explained below.

A second methodological issue involves the problem of grading service-learning requirements. For instance, in a study by Markus et al. (1993), which reported evidence that service-learning augments the mastery of course concepts, students who received regular instruction were "required to write longer term papers based on library research . . ." (p. 412). In criticizing this approach, Miller (1994) points out that, when different requirements are used, it is difficult to rule out the possibility that the criteria for grading service-learning assignments were less rigorous than those used in grading traditional assignments.

Third, on a related issue, there is a need to control for the possibility of grader bias. To the extent that some academic requirements for service-learning students differ from requirements for regular students, the results for the two groups are difficult to compare, and it is not possible to control for the methodological problem of grader bias. For instance, in the study by Kendrick (1996), service-learning students wrote essays centered around their service agency, whereas students in regular instruction wrote essays reflecting upon news articles. Although the results suggested that service-learning students were superior to regular students in the application of course concepts, Kendrick admits that the possible influence of grader bias was not ruled out systematically. In short, the grader of written essays should be *blind* regarding students' group membership in studies of service-learning.

Fourth, another methodological issue involves the way in which students are placed in service-learning vs. regular instruction sections. One approach is to designate one section of a course as requiring a service-learning component, with another section using regular classroom instruction only (Kendrick, 1996). Although this approach is relatively easy to implement, one problem is that it may be difficult to control for differences between the sections in regard to how course concepts are presented in lectures. For instance, one may speculate that, when all students in a particular section are involved in course-related service, the instructor may have a tendency to illustrate course concepts with service-related examples or to vary lectures (or classroom activities) in other ways that influence students' learning. Although researchers utilizing this approach often note that they made the two sections of the course as similar as possible (e.g., Kendrick, 1996), it is unclear whether such classroom dynamics occur.

Random assignment of students to service-learning or regular instruction sections of the course represents another approach to placement (Markus et al., 1993). Although this approach may minimize self-selection biases, the random assignment procedure may introduce controversies regarding the seemingly contradictory notion of *mandatory volunteerism* (see Evers, 1990), and it may not be a feasible practice in many institutions (see Holland, 1997). Due to these issues, very few service-learning outcome studies use the random assignment procedure.

Still another strategy for placement is to provide a service-learning opportunity to students enrolled in the same section of a course (e.g., Miller, 1994). One way of implementing this strategy is to require students who pursue service-learning to enroll in a fourth (service-learning) credit, which subsumes the requirements (academic and service) associated with the service-learning opportunity. This placement strategy allows: (a) an independent grading of students' performance on service-learning vs. traditional course components; (b) a comparison of academic performance of service-learning students vs. regular students on common academic requirements; (c) an assurance that all students are exposed to the same lectures and classroom activities; and (d) an examination of the ways in which students who pursue service-learning differ from those who decline the opportunity.

Within this approach, a researcher could attempt to control for the influence of self-selection biases. However, (a) *"the variables to be controlled are almost infinite . . ."* (Hesser, 1995, p. 34), (b) the use of statistical procedures (e.g., analysis of covariance) to control for variables decreases statistical power, (c) it is unclear which variables are most important to control, and (d) there is disagreement as to how to control those variables that are thought by some to be important. For example, in an attempt to control for general tendencies in academic performance, one could use grade point average (GPA) as a covariate, but such an approach could turn out to be a meaningless endeavor. For the following reasons, the relevance of GPA to the academic performance in a particular course may vary wildly across students enrolled in the course: (a) students in a course have different majors, and level of difficulty of academic requirements varies across disciplines; (b) the level of interest that a student has in a particular course may be greater or less than his or her typical interest level in past courses; and (c) since students in a course are at different academic levels, GPA may be based on one academic year (or less) in some cases and three academic years (or more) in others. Given this background, it would appear that a major concern is whether or not a fine-grained examination of academic performance identifies the following hypothesized pattern: (a) early in the semester, service-learning students and traditional students will exhibit similar levels of academic performance; and (b) as the semester progresses, and service-learning students become more involved in course-relevant service, they will show increasingly superior performance relative to regular students.

To summarize, researchers examining the influence of service-learning on academic performance have used three different strategies for placing students, including: (1) random assignment of students to service-learning or regular instruction sections of a course; (2) designation of one section of a course as including a service-learning component, with another section using regular instruction; and (3) providing an opportunity for service-learning to students enrolled in the same section of a course. The study reported in the present paper utilized the latter placement strategy. Given that: (a) there are methodological pros and cons associated with each strategy, (b) some strategies may be more feasible than others in many academic institutions, and (c) research on service-learning is at a very early developmental stage, it is argued that all of these strategies are appropriate in this area of research. It is believed that, as data accumulate across studies using different research designs, the findings will yield a pattern that clarifies the effects of service-learning on students' mastery of course material.

Finally, another recommendation in the literature is that ". . . evaluations of learning outcomes should test for those types of learning best imparted by service-learning experiences" (Kendrick, 1996, pp. 79-80). As Miller (1994, p. 34) argued, "Traditional in-class graded assignments and tests do not generally tap what successful community service learning experience seems most positively to affect: first hand knowledge of the real world . . ." In some studies indicating that service-learning students and non-service-learning students learned course material at similar levels, service-learning students were found to obtain higher scores on a post-semester questionnaire assessing perceived ability to apply course-related knowledge to the real world (Kendrick, 1996). Service-learning researchers are just beginning to discuss ways of assessing relevant domains of learning (see Driscoll et al., 1996).

One of the authors has coordinated an ongoing service-learning project in his Abnormal Psychology course at the University of Dayton since the Fall semester of 1996. This paper presents outcome data associated with the goals of the project. One goal of the project is to enhance the students' academic benefits, including mastery of standard course material and ability to apply course-related material to real-life situations. It was hypothesized that, as service-learning students became more involved in course-related service, they would show increasingly superior academic performance relative to non-service-learning students. In addition, service-learning students were expected to obtain higher scores than traditional students on a post-semester course evaluation, which assesses students' perceptions in such areas as: (a) level of learning in the course; (b) ability to apply course concepts to new situations; (c) interest and motivation in the course; (d) personal development in the course; and (e) quality of the instructor.

A second goal of the present project is to improve the student's sense of social responsibility, which refers to perceptions of citizenship obligations, awareness of social injustices, and commitment to promote social justice. It was hypothesized that, relative to students who did not pursue the service-learning opportunity, service-learning students would (a) obtain higher scores on a measure of social responsibility at pre-semester, (b) show a pre- to post-semester increase on the social responsibility measure, and (c) obtain a higher score on a post-semester inventory that assesses the course's influence on the development of social responsibility in students.

A third goal of the current service-learning project is to make a clinically significant impact in the community; more specifically, this project attempts to contribute to the psychosocial rehabilitation of troubled youth in the juvenile justice system. Although a major challenge in the area of service-learning is to demonstrate that projects yield educational and community benefits concurrently, researchers have ". . . only begun thinking about the process of assessing community impact" (Driscoll et al., 1996, p. 67). This paper will present preliminary evidence that the project yields clinically significant benefits to the service agency. In addition, a brief description of innovations to be implemented in this service-learning project will be provided.

METHOD

Participants

The participants in this study were 125 undergraduate students who were enrolled in an Abnormal Psychology course during the 1996-1997 academic year. Among the 125 students, 32 pursued service-learning, whereas 93 declined the opportunity. As shown below, service-learning and regular students were roughly equivalent on most demographic variables.

Regarding age, service-learning students (M = 19 years- 11 months, SD = 1 year-2 months) were similar to traditional students (M = 20 years-8 months, SD = 3 years-10 months). The service-learning students consisted of 3 (9%) males and 29 (91%) females, whereas the regular students consisted of 33 (35%) males and 60 (65%) females, suggesting that females were more likely to pursue service-learning. In regard to race/ethnicity, the service-learning students included 31 (97%) European-Americans and 1 (3%) African-American; similarly, the regular students included 81 (87%) European-Americans, 5 (5%) African-Americans, 2 (2%) Asian Americans, and 1 (1%) student not disclosing race/ethnicity. Regarding religious affiliation, the service-learning students included 23 (72%) Catholic students, 6 (19%) Protestant students, and 3 (9%) individuals reporting no religious affiliation; the regular students included 53 (58%) Catholic students, 19 (20%) Protestant students, 2 (2%) Jewish students, and 19 (20%) individuals reporting no affiliation.

Procedures used in the Fall and Spring semesters were identical, and so data were collapsed across semesters for statistical analysis. In support of this decision, service-learning students in the Fall and Spring semesters did not differ on their examination performance, self-reported social responsibility, or post-semester course evaluations. Likewise, regular students in the Fall and Spring semesters did not differ on their examination performance, self-reported social responsibility, or post-semester course evaluations.

The Service Agency

Students in this service-learning project work at Building Bridges, which is a human renewal program for troubled youth involved in the Montgomery County Juvenile Court. As the Building Bridges brochure indicates, "Youngsters are referred to our program as an alternative to long-term confinement . . ." Many of these adolescents meet formal criteria for such conditions as Attention Deficit Hyperactivity Disorder or Conduct Disorder. Service-learning students working at Building Bridges have a number of opportunities for experiential learning, such as tutoring adolescents, supervising adolescents in a *work therapy* program, paraprofessional (supportive) counseling, or assisting Juvenile Probation Officers in case management. The Building Bridges brochure explains that, "The heart of the program . . . depends upon community support, since by law the County is permitted to pay only for probation staff salaries."

Procedure and Materials

At the beginning of the semester, students enrolled in Abnormal Psychology sign an *Informed Consent Document* and complete a *Background/Demographic Questionnaire* if they are willing to participate. The course syllabus, which is distributed on the first day of class, indicates an opportunity to sign up for an additional (fourth) service-learning credit. Interested students attend an orientation meeting in order to: (a) learn more about Building Bridges, (b) view a video-tape of peers describing the value of service-learning, (c) learn about the expectations for students, and (d) discuss implementation details (e.g., transportation). Students who pursue the opportunity complete a *Service-Learning Contract,* which indicates an agreement to: (a) attend orientation meetings at the service agency, (b) work a minimum of three hours per week at the agency, (c) respond to reflection questions via e-mail and group discussions, and (d) write a more extensive paper (relative to the regular requirement) that illustrates course concepts through experiential work.

At pre- and post-semester, all students complete the *Social Responsibility Inventory* (SRI; Markus et al., 1993), which is a 15-item self-report scale assessing perceptions regarding obligations of citizenship, awareness of social injustices, and interest in working toward social equity. Based on the procedure of Markus et al. (1993), participants rated each item on a Likert-like scale ranging from 1 ("not important" or "strongly disagree") to 4 ("essential" or "strongly agree"). The post-semester SRI includes additional items assessing students' perceptions of the course's influence on their views of service. Each of these items were rated on a Likert-like scale ranging from 1 ("not at all") to 4 ("a great deal"). In this study, Chronbach's coefficient alpha for the SRI was .86.

At post-semester, students completed a *Course Evaluation* developed by the *Center for Research on Learning and Teaching* (CRLT) at the University of Michigan (Markus et al., 1993). This instrument assesses students' perceptions in the following areas: (a) level of learning in the course; (b) ability to apply course concepts to new situations; (c) interest and motivation in the course; (d) personal development in the course; and (e) quality of the instructor. Students used a Likert-like scale ranging from 1 ("strongly disagree") to 5 ("strongly agree") to rate these items. Chronbach's coefficient alpha for the CRLT was .88 in this study.

Regarding academic performance, each of four exams consisted of 45 multiple choice items (90%) and one essay (10%). Multiple choice items were computer scored, and the grader of essays was *blind* to group membership. Exams were *objective* in the sense that: (a) items focused on standard course material (i.e., no items were specifically relevant to the service), and (b) items were not qualitatively different from those used in exams prior to implementation of the project. Term papers written by regular students were based on library research, whereas the papers written by service-learning students integrated library research and service-learning experiences. Due to this qualitative difference in paper requirements, there was no attempt to compare the two groups on this variable. As noted earlier, one methodological problem in past studies involved attempts to compare the academic performance of service-learning students vs. regular students on assignments in which requirements differed for the two groups (Miller, 1994).

A *Survey of Clinical Benefits* (SCB) was constructed for supervisors at the service agency to complete in an anonymous fashion. The SCB consists of 10 items assessing supervisors' perceptions of students' clinical contributions to the agency. The five agency supervisors completed the items using a Likert-like scale ranging from 1 ("strongly disagree") to 7 ("strongly agree").

Given the dearth of evidence on the community benefits of service-learning projects, Driscoll et al. (1996) recommended the survey method as a meaningful starting point.

RESULTS

Mastery of Course-Related Concepts

Averaged across Exams I through IV, the service-learning students performed at a higher level than did regular students (M = 84.27, SD = 7.62 vs. M = 81.16, SD = 10.33), t(110) = 1.50, p = .05. Given this general group difference, we employed more specific analyses in order to examine our *a priori* hypothesis regarding the pattern of group differences. Our *a priori* hypothesis was that: (a) service-learning students and regular students would exhibit similar levels of performance early in the semester; and (b) relative to traditional students, service-learning students would show increasingly superior academic performance as their involvement in service increased. As shown below, the results were consistent with this *a priori* hypothesis.

On *Exam I*, the group difference in performance was in the expected direction but not statistically significant (M = 76.48, SD = 10.27 vs. M = 74.21, SD = 11.26), t(118) = 1.00, p = .32. This finding was not surprising given that service-learning students were in an early stage of experiential work at the time of *Exam I*. On *Exam II*, however, the group difference was in the expected direction and closely approached the .05 probability level (M = 88.42, SD = 8.29 vs. M = 85.60, SD = 11.22), t(123) = 1.26, p = .07. Further, the group difference on *Exam III* (M = 90.92, SD = 8.61 vs. M = 87.35, SD = 11.10), t(123) = 1.64, p = .05, and *Exam IV* (M = 82.34, SD = 10.76 vs. M = 76.60, SD = 15.57), t(123) = 2.29, p = .03, was in the expected direction and statistically significant.

On a *Course Evaluation Battery* (Markus et al., 1993), service-learning students gave higher ratings, t(123) = 3.35, p = .001. As shown in Table 1, service-learning students had higher scores on items assessing: (a) level of learning (item 16); (b) ability to apply course concepts to new situations (item 2); (c) interest and motivation (items 5, 9, 12, 14, 17); (d) personal development (items 4, 6, 8, and 10); and (e) quality of the instructor (items 3, 5, 7, and 9).

Social Responsibility

SRI scores (Table 2) for service-learning students at pre-semester (M = 3.11, SD = .30) were significantly higher than the corresponding scores for

TABLE 1. Post-Semester Mean Course Ratings as a Function of Group

	Group	
Course Evaluation Items	Service-Learning (n = 32)	Traditional (n = 93)
1. Overall, the instructor is an excellent teacher.	4.06 (.80)	3.85 (.89)
2. I learned to apply principles from this course to new situations.	4.31* (.78)	3.80 (.83)
3. The instructor delivered clear, organized explanations.	4.44* (.71)	4.15 (.85)
4. I developed a set of overall values in this field.	3.97* (.82)	3.37 (.92)
5. The instructor made the class interesting.	4.00* (.80)	3.55 (1.02)
6. I developed a greater awareness of societal problems.	3.94 (.84)	3.73 (.75)
7. The instructor showed a genuine concern for students.	4.31 (.99)	4.01 (.97)
8. I reconsidered many of my former attitudes.	3.19** (.89)	2.88 (.99)
9. The instructor motivates me to do my best work.	3.66* (.87)	3.19 (.99)
10. I developed a greater sense of personal responsibility.	3.38** (.79)	3.10 (.92)
11. This course required more work than others of equal credit.	3.16* (1.11)	2.73 (1.14)
12. I feel that I am performing up to my potential in this course.	3.81* (1.09)	3.25 (1.27)
13. The grading system was clearly defined.	4.53** (.67)	4.32 (.68)
14. I deepened my interest in the subject matter of this course.	4.34* (.97)	3.95 (.92)
15. Grading was a fair assessment of my performance in this class.	4.19 (1.17)	4.17 (.71)
16. I learned a great deal from this course.	4.53* (.80)	4.26 (.70)
17. Reading assignments are interesting and stimulating.	3.66* (1.09)	3.07 (1.10)
18. Examinations cover the important aspects of the course.	4.34* (.70)	3.93 (.87)

Note: *p < .05.
          **p < .10.

Values in parentheses are standard deviations.

regular students (M = 2.89, SD = .35), t(122) = 3.12, p = .002, and this difference was still evident at post-semester (M = 3.17, SD = .32 vs. M = 2.91, SD = .39), t(117) = 3.36, p = .001. As expected, pre- to post-semester changes in SRI scores for regular students were nonsignificant, t(85) = −1.01, p = .32. Given that: (a) the service-learning students' SRI scores were high at pre-semester and (b) the SRI rating scale is restricted (4-point scale), a *ceiling effect* may have precluded an optimal test of the hypothesis that service-learning students' SRI scores would increase from pre- to post-semester. Pre- to post-semester changes in service-learning students' SRI scores were in the expected direction but not statistically significant, t(30) = −1.26, p = .11.

Service-learning and non-service-learning students were also compared on the additional post-semester SRI items that assessed students' perceptions of the course's influence on their views of community service (Table 3). As hypothesized, the scores of service-learning students on these items (M = 3.01, SD = .55) were significantly higher than the scores of regular students (M = 2.44, SD = .67), t(119) = 4.28, p = 001.

Clinical Benefits to Service Agency

Survey and qualitative data suggest that the service-learning students made clinically significant contributions to the service agency. The five supervisors rated each item of the SCB on a Likert-like scale ranging from 1 ("strongly disagree") to 7 ("strongly agree"). The average rating across items was 6.80, with a range of 6.60 to 7.00. Table 4 presents the mean and range of ratings for each survey item.

In support of the survey data, letters written to the first author from Building Bridges staff illustrate the students' meaningful contributions to the service agency. In the Fall semester of 1996, the Director of Building Bridges provided the following comments in a letter:

> I would like to thank you for initiating the field experience in your psychology course. Your students have been instrumental in the implementation of our . . . program for delinquent and "at risk" youth. After talking to some of the college interns, I would say that the benefit appears to be mutual. The interns gain insight and experience, and the youth are provided with mentors, and they receive the attention that they crave and do not receive in their own homes . . . The University of Dayton students have contributed substantially to the success of our treatment program . . .

TABLE 2. Pre-Semester Mean Scores on the Social Responsibility Inventory Function of Group

Social Responsibility Inventory Items	Group Service-Learning (n = 32)	Traditional (n = 93)
1. Working toward equal opportunity for all U.S. citizens.	3.50* (.57)	3.09 (.85)
2. Developing a meaningful philosophy of life.	3.41 (.91)	2.79 (.78)
3. Becoming involved in a program to improve my community.	3.09* (.68)	2.79 (.78)
4. Being very well off financially.	2.41 (.79)	2.20 (.82)
5. Volunteering my time helping people in need.	3.38* (.66)	2.96 (.75)
6. Giving 3% or more of my income to help those in need.	2.91* (.81)	2.39 (.84)
7. Finding a career that provides the opportunity to be helpful to others or useful to society.	3.83* (.45)	3.55 (1.24)
8. Adults should give some time for the good of their community or country.	3.66* (.48)	3.22 (.66)
9. Having an impact on the world is within the reach of most individuals.	3.09 (.85)	2.97 (.84)
10. Most misfortunes that occur to people are frequently the result of circumstances beyond their control.	2.36 (.82)	2.48 (.88)
11. If I could change one thing about society, it would be to achieve greater social justice.	3.09 (.58)	2.92 (.69)
12. I make quick judgments about homeless people.	3.03 (.78)	3.06 (.89)
13. People, regardless of whether they have been successful or not, ought to help those in need.	3.34* (.70)	3.04 (.80)
14. People ought to help those in need as a "payback" for their own opportunities, fortunes, and successes.	2.51* (.96)	2.04 (.99)
15. I feel that I can make a difference in the world.	3.06 (.94)	3.32 (.81)

Note: *$p < .05$.
Values in parentheses are standard deviations.

TABLE 3. Group Differences on Post-Semester Items of the Social Responsibility Scale That Assess the Course's Influence on Students' Social Responsibility

This course increased or strengthened my . . .	Group	
	Service-Learning (*n* = 32)	Traditional (*n* = 93)
1. Intention to serve others in need.	3.38* (.75)	2.48 (.89)
2. Intention to give to charity to help those in need.	2.78* (.83)	1.95 (.94)
3. Sense of purpose or direction in life.	2.94* (.87)	2.34 (.95)
4. Orientation toward others and away from yourself.	2.81** (.85)	2.44 (.87)
5. Intention to work on behalf of social justice.	2.72* (.77)	2.12 (.92)
6. Belief that helping those in need is one's social responsibility.	2.94* (.80)	2.17 (.97)
7. Belief that one can make a difference in the world.	2.81* (.96)	2.22 (.97)
8. Understanding of the role of external forces as shapers of the individual.	3.40 (.66)	3.22 (.85)
9. Tolerance and appreciation of others.	3.28** (.88)	2.96 (.91)

Note: *$p < .01$.
        **$p < .05$.
Values in parentheses are standard deviations.

In the Spring semester of that academic year, the Director of Building Bridges wrote a follow-up letter that included the following comments:

> The collaboration between our agency and your students continues to be of mutual benefit . . . These types of programs give our youth much better odds for success . . . The more proactive programming that is done, the less reactive court intervention that is necessary . . .

In addition, the Coordinator of Education at the service agency provided the following comments to the first author:

> . . . Our youth are involved in the juvenile court. In the majority of cases, they are poor, . . . and were abused . . . and neglected in the past.

Their participation in your program . . . enables them to learn . . . skills and gain experience that would not otherwise be available to them. In today's world, this knowledge is invaluable, even more so to youth who have so many obstacles to overcome to succeed . . . In addition, and of equal importance, the one-on-one personal contact with your students . . . provides each of them with a . . . caring, supportive relationship . . .

DISCUSSION

This paper presents the results of a service-learning project in an Abnormal Psychology course. This ongoing service-learning project has three major goals. The first goal is to enhance the students' academic benefits, including mastery of course material and ability to apply course-related material to real-life situations. Results revealed the following hypothesized pattern of academic performance: at the beginning of the semester, students who pursued service-learning and students who declined the opportunity exhibited similar performance levels on examinations; however, as the semester progressed, and service-learning students became more involved in course-related service, they showed increasingly superior academic performance relative to regular students.

While these findings are consistent with results of some studies (e.g., Giles & Eyler, 1994; Markus et al., 1993), other studies did not find service-learning to augment students' mastery of course material (e.g., Kendrick, 1996; Miller, 1994). In attempting to explain his results, Kendrick (1996) noted that the course examined in his study did not strive to integrate course content and service experiences, whereas past studies reporting positive findings had placed a greater emphasis on integrating conceptual and experiential components. In the present study, there was an emphasis on integrating course content and service-experiences; that is, service-learning students engaged in regular reflection and wrote a comprehensive term paper, and both of these requirements involved examining and illustrating course concepts through experiential work. Thus, we concur with Kendrick's view that level of integration may be an important variable in explaining inconsistent results, but further research is needed to confirm this hypothesis.

The present study controlled for two methodological problems in past research. First, in the present study, service-learning and regular students were exposed to the same lectures (and classroom activities). Second, this study compared the performance of the two groups on the same academic requirements. Third, the examinations used in this study were objective; that is: (a) all items (multiple choice and essay) focused on standard course concepts (i.e., none of the items were directly related to the service), (b) items

TABLE 4. Mean Service Agency Supervisors' Ratings on the Survey of Clinical Benefits

Items of Survey of Clinical Benefits	Mean of Supervisors' Ratings	Range of Supervisors' Ratings
1. Service-learning students serve as positive role models for the youth at Building Bridges.	6.80	6.00 - 7.00
2. Service-learning students make a clinically significant contribution (i.e., a meaningful difference) in this setting.	6.60	6.00 - 7.00
3. Service-learning students work with the staff at Building Bridges in helpful ways (i.e., in ways that help staff members to meet their goals).	6.80	6.00 - 7.00
4. Service-learning students establish meaningful relationships with the youth at Building Bridges.	6.60	5.00 - 7.00
5. Service-learning students influence the youth of Building Bridges in ways that are "therapeutic."	6.80	6.00 - 7.00
6. Service-learning students help the youth of Building Bridges to help themselves.	6.90	6.50 - 7.00
7. At Building Bridges, service-learning students apply knowledge in ways that help in resolving "real-life" problems.	6.80	6.00 - 7.00
8. Service-learning students establish good working relationships with the staff at Building Bridges.	6.80	6.00 - 7.00
9. The youth at Building Bridges benefit in real ways from working with service-learning students.	6.90	6.50 - 7.00
10. Overall, it is very important to Building Bridges that this service-learning project continue.	7.00	7.00 - 7.00

Note: To rate items of the Survey of Clinical Benefits, supervisors used a Likert-like scale ranging 1 ("strongly disagree") to 7 ("strongly agree").

were not qualitatively different from those used in this course before the project was implemented, (c) 90% of the items on each examination were multiple choice and computer scored, and (d) the grader of the essay (worth 10%) on each examination was *blind* to group membership. However, one limitation of the present study is that the influence of self-selection biases on the results cannot be ruled out. Although we need more studies that randomly assign the students to service-learning or regular instruction (see Markus et al., 1993), researchers must be careful to circumvent the potential problems associated with requiring community service (see Evers, 1990).

Results from a post-semester course evaluation suggested that, relative to traditional students, students who pursued service-learning were more likely to perceive themselves as having learned to apply course concepts to new situations. This finding is consistent with the results of other studies (e.g., Markus et al., 1993; Kendrick, 1996). The importance of this type of learning is evident; as noted by Miller (1994, p. 34), " . . . helping students to be able to successfully apply knowledge to the real world, and not just to understand concepts in a way that is measured by traditional tests, is a basic and critical goal of education . . . " However, in all relevant studies in the literature, including this one, the examination of whether service-learning produced this benefit was based solely on students' perceptions. While students' perceptions represent one important dimension, there is a need to assess service-learning students' "first hand knowledge of the real world . . . " in a more comprehensive fashion (Miller, 1994, p. 34). In future studies, for instance, it may be possible to assess students' knowledge of: (a) the juvenile justice system, (b) the interrelationship between this system and the mental health system, (c) the comorbidity between Attention-Deficit Hyperactivity Disorder and Conduct Disorder, or (d) the ways in which social injustices contribute to the development of juvenile delinquency.

The second goal of this ongoing project is to promote in students the development of social responsibility. Service-learning students had very high SRI scores at pre-semester and, therefore, a ceiling effect may have precluded an optimal examination of pre- to post-semester changes in SRI scores. In future studies, the range of the Likert-like scale used by students to rate SRI items should be increased. Nevertheless, on additional post-semester SRI items that assess students' perceptions of the course's influence on their views of service, service-learning students obtained higher scores than did traditional students. Thus, results provide some support for the hypothesis that service-learning promotes a sense of social responsibility, and this finding is consistent with most other studies in the literature (e.g., Batchelder & Root, 1994; Kendrick, 1996; Markus et al., 1993; McClusky-Fawcett & Green, 1992).

A third goal of the service-learning project is to make clinically significant contributions to the psychosocial rehabilitation of troubled youth in the juvenile justice system. Preliminary data provide tentative evidence that service-learning students make meaningful contributions. Given the absence of research examining the community benefits, the survey results and qualitative data reported in the present paper represent a meaningful beginning (Driscoll et al., 1996), but future research must move toward a more systematic and comprehensive evaluation of the contribution of service-learning projects to the service agencies.

Innovations to be implemented in this project are guided in part by Boyer's (1994) philosophical vision of a "New American College." First, the service agency (Building Bridges) will be interfaced with the Learning Village at the University of Dayton, so that institutional resources (e.g., computers) can be utilized in service provision. At the University of Dayton, the Learning Village supports faculty in their efforts to "extend learning beyond the traditional notions of classroom instruction by incorporating campus life, community service, and professional experiences into an active and rich learning process . . ." Second, collaborations between students and community professionals will be arranged. Thus far, professionals from the following sites have made a commitment to collaborate: AIDS Foundation of Miami Valley; Dayton City Police DARE (Drug Abuse Resistance Education) Program; and the Sinclair Community College's Experience-Based Education Program. Third, program evaluation will be extended to include a pre- to post-intervention assessment of clinical benefits in the following areas: (a) academic achievement and literacy; (b) computer literacy; (c) AIDS knowledge and risk behavior; (d) risk for substance abuse; and (e) self-concept. Finally, the evaluation of educational benefits to service-learning students will continue, allowing a determination of the extent to which these educational benefits become more *potent* as innovations in the project are implemented.

REFERENCES

Batchhelder, T. H., & Root, S. (1994). Effects of an undergraduate program to integrate academic learning and service: Cognitive, prosocial cognitive, and identity outcomes. *Journal of Adolescence, 17*, 341-355.

Boyer, E. (1994, March 9). Creating the New American College. *The Chronicle of Higher Education*: A48.

Bringle, R. G., & Kremer, J. F. (1993). Evaluation of an intergenerational service-learning project for undergraduates. *Educational Gerontology, 19*, 407-416.

Cohen, J., & Kinsey, D. (1994). "Doing good" and scholarship: A service-learning study. *Journalism Educator*, 4-14.

Driscoll, A., Holland, B., Gelmon, S., & Kerrigan, S. (1996). An assessment model for service-learning: Comprehensive case studies of impact on faculty, students, community and institution. *Michigan Journal of Community Service Learning, 3*, 66-71.

Evers, W. M. (1990). *National service: Pro and con.* Stanford, CA: Hoover Institution Press.

Giles, D. E., & Eyler, J. (1994). The impact of a college community service laboratory on students' personal, social, and cognitive outcomes. *Journal of Adolescence, 17,* 327-329.

Hesser, G. (1995). Faculty assessment of student learning: Outcomes attributed to service-learning and evidence of changes in faculty attitudes about experiential education. *Michigan Journal of Community Service Learning, 2,* 33-42.

Holland, B. (1997). Analyzing institutional commitment to service: A model of key organizational factors. *Michigan Journal of Community Service Learning, 4,* 30-41.

Kendrick, J. R. (1996). Outcomes of service-learning in an Introduction to Sociology course. *Michigan Journal of Community Service Learning, 3,* 72-81.

Markus, G. B., Howard, J., & King, D. C. (1993). Integrating community service and classroom instruction enhances learning: Results from an experiment. *Educational Evaluation and Policy Analysis, 15,* 410-419.

McCluskey-Fawcett, K., & Green, P. (1992). Using community service to teach developmental psychology. *Teaching Psychology, 19,* 150-152.

Miller, J. (1994). Linking traditional and service-learning courses: Outcome evaluations utilizing two pedagogically distinct models. *Michigan Journal of Community Service Learning, 1* 29-36.

Olney, C., & Grande, S. (1995). Validation of a scale to measure development of social responsibility. *Michigan Journal of Community Service Learning, 2,* 43-53.

Sugar, J., & Livosky, M. (1988). Enriching child psychology courses with a preschool journal option. *Teaching of Psychology, 15,* 93-95.

Faculty and Student Participation and Perceptions of Service-Learning Outcomes

M. Michelle Rowe
Judith G. Chapman

Saint Joseph's University

SUMMARY. Faculty (n = 55) and student (n = 75) perceptions of service-learning outcomes were evaluated using a questionnaire format. Results indicated that while faculty strongly believe service-learning is important to student academic growth, few actually teach service-learning courses because of time constraints and unfamiliarity with service-learning course models. Comparisons of faculty and student perceptions showed that compared to students, faculty had a stronger perception of the value of service-learning for students. When students were divided into those who had (n = 33) or had not (n = 42) participated in service-learning, faculty and service-learning students' perceptions did not differ, and both rated these experiences more valuable than did non-service-learning students. *[Article copies available for a fee from The Haworth Document Delivery Service: 1-800-342-9678. E-mail address: getinfo@haworthpressinc.com]*

Address correspondence to: M. Michelle Rowe, Department of Health Services, Saint Joseph's University, 5600 City Avenue, Philadelphia, PA 19131 (E-mail: mrowe@sju.edu).

The authors thank Dr. Julie M. McDonald for her assistance with data collection, and Sr. Frances Hart, Ms. Kathy McCauley, Ms. Connie McSherry, and Sr. Francis Joseph of the Faith-Justice Institute for their helpful suggestions on the instrumentation and data collection procedures.

[Haworth co-indexing entry note]: "Faculty and Student Participation and Perceptions of Service-Learning Outcomes." Rowe, M. Michelle, and Judith G. Chapman. Co-published simultaneously in *Journal of Prevention & Intervention in the Community* (The Haworth Press, Inc.) Vol. 18, No. 1/2, 1999, pp. 83-96; and: *Educating Students to Make-a-Difference: Community-Based Service Learning* (ed: Joseph R. Ferrari, and Judith G. Chapman) The Haworth Press, Inc., 1999, pp. 83-96. Single or multiple copies of this article are available for a fee from The Haworth Document Delivery Service [1-800-342-9678, 9:00 a.m. - 5:00 p.m. (EST). E-mail address: getinfo@haworthpressinc.com].

83

Societal issues such as physical and psychological illness are increasingly more difficult to manage given the current health care system, and most health care professionals would agree that treatment of a disease or disorder cannot be done during office visits alone. Illness is typically a manifestation of a larger societal problem (Costa & VandenBos, 1990)–issues of family abuse, depression, and alcoholism are generally a consequence of dysfunctional family and societal systems, and the rates of widespread illnesses such as cardiac disease, AIDS, and stress-related disorders are increasing yearly (Edlin, Golanty, McCormack Brown, 1997).

Indeed, society plays a significant role in both the definition of the illness and the success of treatment. In fact, it has been observed that illness is socially constructed through processes that include: identifying the origin of the illness, assessing responsibility for the illness, assigning guilt or innocence to the victim of the illness, and assigning responsibility for a cure (Herek & Glunt, 1988; Marlatt & Gordon, 1985). If it is the case that society socially constructs illness, we can socially reconstruct it through a series of processes: (a) Society must be educated formally about the illness process, (b) society must be involved with victims of illness, and (c) society must share these experiences. One way to initiate this process is by exposing undergraduate students to community issues as part of their academic experiences through service-learning. Students who participate in service-learning combine community service with formal study, providing an opportunity for them to reflect on classroom theories in relation to field experiences, and enabling them to employ systematic and creative methods when seeking solutions to problems.

Human services fields have become increasingly dependent on volunteerism and citizen participation in the past several decades (Sharon, 1991). Reliance on volunteer services has meet needs: (a) to make up for reductions in publicly and privately funded programs, (b) to humanize services that have become impersonal and bureaucratic, (c) to provide constructive outlets for individuals who have excess leisure time, and (d) to generally improve community and societal conditions by involving lay citizens (Sharon, 1991). Consequently, homeless shelters and food banks, literacy programs, community youth centers, and public health programs utilize a growing number of young adults who assist human service providers, with the most active group typically being students. In fact, prior research has shown that nearly two of three incoming college students have participated in some form of volunteer work during the previous academic year (Astin 1984; Serow, 1991).

While most Americans endorse the importance of volunteerism, only about one-third actually volunteer some of their free time to help others (Independent Sector, 1988; 1992). Research on the primary reasons why people participate in community service suggests that volunteers want to help others, to contribute to the community, to obtain training and skills, to enrich their personal lives, to be needed, to make new friends and be around others, to explore career options, to correct social problems, and to demonstrate behavior consistent with religious beliefs (Independent Sector, 1981; Serow, 1991). In addition to satisfying a number of personal needs, volunteer activity has been shown to reflect a high level of social interest–an interest in the general concerns of mankind (Ansbaucher, 1968; Crandall & Harris, 1976; Hettman & Jenkins, 1990).

Recent goals of higher education have focused on the education of the 'whole' student in the context of the total educational environment (Miller & Prince, 1976). Several studies have demonstrated the importance of a balanced, integrated environment and suggest that the more highly involved students are in campus activities, the greater their persistence, satisfaction, and achievement in college (Astin, 1984; Fitch, 1991). Service-learning, the integration of community-service and academic curriculum, is one type of activity believed to promote care, compassion, and responsibility in college students. Supporters of service-learning view community service experiences as a worthwhile extension to more conventional forms of civic and moral education. Consequently, research on the psychological outcomes of students who participate in service-learning consistently has demonstrated meaningful benefits (Palestini, Rowe, & Chapman, 1997) for students, including social awareness, social responsibility, and concern for others. In addition, service can provide opportunities to acquire interpersonal skills, proficiency in time management, and feelings of general competency on the part of student volunteers (Serow, Ciechalski, & Daye, 1990). Finally, participating students have the opportunity within a structured and supervised environment to address some of society's serious problems (Clary, Synder, Ridge, Miene, & Haugen, 1994; Rowe, Palestini, & Chapman, 1997; Palestini, Rowe, & Chapman, 1997).

A commitment to service in surrounding communities by colleges and universities is critical for several reasons. First, students need to find relevance between what is learned in the classroom and what is experienced in life. This might reduce the tendency on the part of some to see higher education as "an ivory tower of irrelevance" (Eby, 1995). Second, educators should take an active role in providing experiences that align knowledge and responsibility to produce civic minded citizens who are not only intelligent and responsible, but caring and compassionate. Students should be responsible not only for learning course material but for developing skills that will allow them to make appropriate decisions, skills which are developed when theory meets experience. Third, faculty involved in higher education cultivate new ideas, new ways of looking at problems, and new solutions to these problems. Service-learning provides institutions a way to apply a wealth of intellect, research findings, and resources to find solutions to challenging societal problems, and may show students that each person can make a difference.

In order for service-learning to be effective, it should be integrated developmentally across the curriculum. For example, in our undergraduate major, "Interdisciplinary Health Services" (a program of study which combines the natural sciences, social sciences, liberal arts courses, and health-related curriculum), the first service-learning experience will focus on the ways in which society perceives and responds to people with illnesses and disabilities. The purpose of this initial experience is to raise *social awareness.* The second level of exposure will focus on how factors such as race, class, and gender shape physical and mental illness. Here, the emphasis of service-learning is on *social analysis.* During the third service-learning experience, students concentrate on the *ethical and legal* aspects of the health care system. The final step is a capstone experience and research project incorporating each of the prior three components. The emphases is on the development of *leadership and creative problem solving* techniques as students are expected to identify, research, and suggest a solution to a health care problem.

Service-learning experiences take a variety of forms and can include the following: (a) Service-learning as a *Form of Scholarship* provides opportunities for structured reflection by combining classroom cognition and experiential knowledge, resulting in increases in student concern for civic values and service ethics (Eby, 1995); (b) *Peer Teaching,* the use of cooperative learning and academic interventions, has been demonstrated to be valuable for both the "teacher" and the "learner." In particular, students report a sense of freedom to express opinions and ask questions. More importantly, the development of metacognitive strategies resulting from the interactions between students is found more frequently than with traditional classroom methods (Vaidya & Clark, 1995); (c) *Community Literacy* engages students as literacy mentors. Since this typically involves a boundary crossing of race and socioeconomic status, students develop a respect for, and appreciation of differences between individuals along with a sense of social action and responsibility (Long, 1995); (d) *Intergenerational Community Projects* match students with older adults from public housing communities and has been shown to provide a sense of empowerment in solving social problems and a greater understanding of individual differences (Ward & McCrea, 1995); (e) *Child Mentor Programs,* in which students teach skills such as reading or mathematics to children, provides social support and friendship, increases students' sense of self-esteem and social values as well as mastery of the content area (Huwar, 1995); and (f) *Off-Campus Immersion Programs* involve off-campus volunteering usually during semester breaks. These projects vary depending upon the site, but generally consist of living and working with recipients of the service project. Examples include building low-cost housing or a community playground and clean-up projects. Because students are immersed in the culture of their recipients, they report high levels of personal growth and a sense of control over social inequities (Crowner, 1995).

While the outcomes of service-learning are clearly beneficial to both the students and society, service-learning must be valued by students, faculty, and administrators alike to ensure program success. If faculty do not believe in the importance or value of service-learning, if they do not have administrative support, or if their schedules are too overwhelming, service-learning simply becomes another great idea that does advance. The purposes of this study were: (a) To examine and compare perceptions of the impact of service-learning experiences between faculty and students, (b) to identify and evaluate the reasons why faculty do or do not include a service-learning component in their courses; and (c) to determine what information faculty require in order to consider including a service-learning component in their courses.

METHOD

Participants

A total of 55 faculty and 75 students served as participants. Faculty departments varied and included Aerospace Studies, Biology, Business, Chemistry, Economics, Education, English, Fine Arts and Performing Arts, Foreign Languages and Literatures, Health Services, History, Math, Philosophy, Physics, Political Science, Psychology, Sociology, and Theology. The faculty were grouped by academic division into Social Sciences ($n = 16$), Humanities ($n = 16$), Natural Sciences ($n = 8$), and Business ($n = 12$). The number of years of teaching experience averaged 13.44 ($SD = 10.71$), and all faculty held full-time tenure-track lines for at least one year. Few ($n = 11$; 20%) reported teaching service-learning courses.

Students were enrolled full-time and were taking an introductory philosophy course which fulfilled a general education requirement for graduation. Thirty-three students were enrolled in a service-learning section of the course while the remaining 42 students were in a nonservice-learning section taught by the same instructor.

Materials and Procedures

All faculty and students completed an eight item scale, the *Service-Learning Outcomes Scale,* that asked them to indicate their perceptions of students who had participated in service-learning courses as compared to students who had not. Each item was answered on a 5-point rating scale (with end-points being 1 = strongly agree, and 5 = strongly disagree), with individual items asking participants to compare service-learning and non-service-learning students they have encountered on: (a) their understanding of social problems, (b) the richness of their educational experiences, (c) their perceived efficacy to make the world a better place, (d)) their level of self-esteem, (e) their ability to solve problems, (f) their potential to be future leaders, (g) their level of compassion, and (h) their sensitivity to social inequities. Scale items were generated by the authors based on prior research identifying the outcomes of service-learning for students (Astin, 1984; Fitch, 1991; Clary, Snyder, Ridge, Miene, & Haugen, 1994; Rowe, Palestini, & Chapman, 1997; Palestini, Rowe, & Chapman, 1997).

The questionnaires completed by faculty included two additional sections. Section II presented five dichotomous forced-choice items (Yes-No) that asked whether or not: (a) they taught a service-learning course, (b) a service-learning component was appropriate given their course content, (c) they would teach a service-learning course if they had more time, (d) they would teach a service-learning course if they had more information about how to do it, and (e) they had served as a mentor in any other type of community service program.

Section III of the faculty questionnaire included qualitative items which asked faculty why they do or do not teach a service-learning course, and if they did not, what they would like to know about service-learning in order that they might decide to offer a service-learning course. In addition, this section included demographic items (e.g., major discipline and number of years of teaching).

Questionnaires were sent to 138 full-time, tenure-track faculty through inter-office mail at the beginning of the first week of November. Faculty were provided with an introductory letter requesting their participation and describing the purpose of the research. Instructions appeared on the questionnaire, which took approximately 15 minutes to complete. Faculty were given one month to return the completed questionnaires, and were sent an e-mail reminder to do so two weeks after the questionnaires had been mailed. A total of 55 questionnaires were returned, resulting in a response rate of 40%.

The questionnaires were distributed to students during regular class time at the end of the semester (last week of November). Students were provided with an informed consent letter which specified the purpose of the research, the rights of human subjects, and the name and address of the Human Subjects Committee Chair. Instructions appeared at the top of the scale which took approximately 10 minutes of class time for all students to complete.

RESULTS

Service-Learning Outcomes Scale

Means and standard deviations of individual scale item responses are presented in Table 1 for faculty, all students, and service-learning and nonservice-learning student groups. Separate one-way analyses of variance were conducted on each of the outcome items to determine whether there were differences in perceived outcomes as a function of the faculty's academic division [Social Sciences (n = 16), Humanities (n = 16), Natural Sciences (n = 8), and Business (n = 12)]. No significant differences between divisions emerged on items suggesting service-learning students have a better understanding of social problems, have richer educational experiences, have greater perceived efficacy to make the world a better place, have higher self-esteem, or have greater potential to be future leaders. There were significant differences between faculty of different divisions in perceptions of service-learning students as better problem solvers, $F(3,48)$ = 3.84, p < .05. A post-hoc Tukey HSD test demonstrated that Humanities faculty (M = 4.13, SD = 0.81) and Business faculty (M = 3.83, SD = 0.84) had stronger perceptions of the problem solving capacity of service-learning students than faculty from the Natural Sciences (M = 3.0, SD = 0.54). There were also significant differences between faculty of different divisions in perceptions of level of compassion of service-learning compared to nonservice-learning students, $F(3,48)$ = 2.95, p < .01. A Tukey HSD test demonstrated that Business faculty (M = 4.92, SD = 0.30) had stronger perceptions of the compassion of service-learning students than the Social Science faculty (M = 4.19, SD = 0.75), and both Business and Humanities faculty (M = 4.56, SD = 0.63) had stronger perceptions than faculty in the Natural Sciences (M = 3.75, SD = 0.89). Finally, significant differences in perceptions emerged on the item assessing sensitivity of service-learning students, $F(3,48)$ = 3.07, p < .05. A Tukey HSD test demonstrated that Humanities faculty (M = 4.69, SD = 0.70) and Business faculty (M = 4.67, SD = 0.65) had more positive perceptions of the sensitivity of service-learning students relative to nonservice-learning students compared to the Natural Science faculty (M = 3.89, SD = 0.64).

Separate t-tests were conducted on each of the perception items to determine whether there were differences in perceptions between faculty and students when comparing service-learning to non-service-learning students. Significant differences between faculty and students were found on each item, with faculty rating the value of service-learning outcomes significantly higher than did students (see Table 1). Specifically, faculty reported that service-learning students, as compared to non-service-learning students, demonstrate: (a) a better understanding of societal problems, $t(128)$ = 3.46, p < .001, (b) richer educational experiences, $t(128)$ = 2.49, p < .05, (c) greater

TABLE 1. Mean Perception Ratings of Service-Learning Outcomes of Faculty and Students

OUTCOME	GROUPS			
	Faculty	Service-Learning Students	Nonservice-Learning Students	Combined Students
Societal Problems	4.42 (066)	4.27 (0.72)	3.74 0.73)	3.97 (0.77)
Richer Educational Experiences	4.35 (0.70)	4.30 (0.81)	3.76 (0.79)	4.00 (0.70)
Greater Efficacy	4.15 (0.80)	3.67 (0.85)	3.71 (0.60)	3.69 (0.71)
Higher Self-Esteem	3.90 (0.81)	3.49 (0.83)	3.29 (0.92)	3.37 (0.88)
Better Problem Solvers	3.71 (0.86)	3.52 (0.76)	3.10 (0.84)	3.27 (0.83)
Future Leaders	3.96 (0.74)	3.70 (1.10)	3.57 (0.86)	3.63 (0.97)
More Compassion	4.38 (0.73)	4.36 (0.90)	3.71 (0.84)	4.00 (0.92)
More Sensitive	4.49 (0.69)	4.52 (0.80)	3.62 (0.94)	4.01 (0.98)

Note: Values in parentheses are standard deviations.

efficacy to make the world a better place, $t(128) = 3.38$, $p < .001$, (d) higher self-esteem, $t(128) = 3.42$, $p < .001$, (e) better problem-solving capacity, $t(128) = 2.97$, $p < .01$, (f) greater propensity to be future leaders, $t(128) = 2.15$, $p < .05$, (g) more compassion, $t(128) = 2.56$, $p < .05$, and (g) more sensitivity, $t(128) = 3.10$, $p < .01$.

Further analyses were done to determine whether there were differences in perceptions of outcomes between the Faculty and each of the student groups, the Service-Learning group, and the Nonservice-Learning group. Post hoc comparisons between the means of each of these groups were done using the Tukey HSD test. Significant differences were found on all items except the item suggesting that service-learning students have greater potential to become future leaders. Both Faculty and Service-Learning students indicated a significantly stronger perception than Nonservice-Learning students that students who participate in service-learning have: (a) a better understanding of societal problems, $F(2,127) = 11.83$, $p < .001$, (b) richer educational experiences, $F(2,127)$ = 8.00, $p < .001$, (c) greater efficacy to make the world a better place, $F(2,127)$ = 5.70, $p < .01$, and (d) higher self-esteem, $F(2,127)$ = 6.36, $p < .01$, compared to students who do not participate in community service. Likewise, Faculty and Service-Learning students reported a stronger belief than Nonservice-Learning students that students who participate in service-learning are: (a) better problem solvers, $F(2,127)$ = 7.24, $p < .001$, (b) more compassionate, $F(2,127)$ = 9.48, $p < .001$, and (c) more sensitive to social inequities, $F(2,127)$ = 17.12, $p < .001$, than are students who do not participate in service-learning.

Dichotomous Items: Faculty Responses

Table 2 presents percentage of respondents indicating yes or no to each of the five dichotomous items on the faculty questionnaire. Percentages are presented for all faculty and faculty by division. It should be noted that chi-square analyses were conducted on the data, and significant differences between the divisions were identified, however, the data did not meet the criteria because more than one-fifth of fitted cells were sparse.

A majority of Social Science, Humanities, and Business faculty felt that service-learning was appropriate for the courses that they taught. Faculty in the Natural Sciences unanimously agreed that course content in the sciences is not appropriate for a service-learning component. Professors in the Social

TABLE 2. Percentages of Responses on Dichotomous Items by Academic Division and All Faculty

Item	Social Sciences (n = 16)		Humanities (n = 16)		Natural Sciences (n = 8)		Business (n = 12)		All Faculty (n = 55)	
	Yes	No	Yes	No	Yes	No	Yes	No	Yes	No
Appropriate to course taught	88	12	75	25	0	100	75	25	60	40
Do you teach SL course	19	81	38	62	0	100	8	92	20	80
If more time would you teach SL	69*	25*	63*	25*	12	88	58*	33*	58*	35*
If more info would you teach SL	50*	44*	63*	19*	38	62	67*	25*	56*	35
Mentor other community service	31	69	19	81	0	100	8	92	16	84

*Some subjects did not respond, thus total does not equal 100%

Sciences, Humanities, and Businesses are currently teaching service-learning courses, with the greatest percentage of faculty teaching these courses in the Humanities. A larger majority of faculty in the Social Sciences, Humanities, and Business indicated their willingness to consider teaching a service-learning course if they had more time to devote to developing the course, with a much smaller percentage of Natural Science faculty indicating the same. A majority of Humanities and Business faculty indicated willingness to teach a service-learning course if they were provided with more information relevant to course development, whereas Social Science faculty were more evenly split on the question, and Natural Science faculty indicated they were not willing to consider the possibility even with more information. Clearly, many Social Science faculty are already involved in service activities with students outside of the classroom, with Humanities faculty indicating some involvement in other community service projects. Whereas Business faculty indicated some involvement, none of the Natural Science faculty responding have served as student mentors in service projects.

Qualitative Items

Separate content analyses were conducted on each of the qualitative items. Of those faculty who reported that they teach service-learning courses ($n = 11$), reasons given for doing so included: (a) to enrich the course content into a multi-leveled experience, (b) to raise the awareness of social issues and social inequities, (c) to provide real world experience (theory into practice–"University life is a very closed world"), (d) to develop student leadership skills, (e) because it is consistent with the mission of the University, and (f) because it should be required for all students.

Of those faculty who reported they do not teach service-learning courses ($n = 45$), reasons for not doing so included: (a) not appropriate to the content area, (b) it involves a major change to the course and curriculum, (c) it creates problems with standardized curriculum between many faculty teaching required large courses, (d) there is not enough time to cover all of the material, (e) priorities of other commitments (research, tenure, promotion), (f) not sure how to do it, (g) it should not be forced upon students, and (h) do not know why not.

Of the faculty who indicated they would like more information about incorporating a service-learning component in their courses ($n = 27$), information requested included: (a) how to balance rigorous academic content with practical experience, (b) how to incorporate service-learning into academic content areas and what fields are best suited for this design, (c) what the University is willing to do to encourage faculty participation (financial, course reductions), and (d) how to actually implement it (site contacts, class sizes, course expectations, amount of time spent at the site).

DISCUSSION

There is reason to believe that service learning can be a powerful tool in infusing or developing a carative spirit in our young people. Educators have long recognized the transforming effect of study abroad. Changing a student's cultural context results in a personal self-evaluation as well as a great deal of learning. The experience of community service, in linking a student to an environment in which knowledge can be put to use and reality can be tested, can have a similarly transforming effect. Given the potential for positive outcomes delineated in this and previous studies, academic programs should be encouraged to include service-learning experiences in the curriculum.

The results of the present study indicate that faculty agree students who participate in service-learning have a better understanding of societal problems, richer educational experiences, are more inclined to become leaders, become more compassionate, and are more sensitive to social inequities as compared to their nonservice-learning peers. However, only a relatively small portion of faculty who responded actually teach service-learning courses. For service-learning programs to be successful, it is imperative that faculty support and encourage students to participate. To facilitate faculty participation, it would be important to provide faculty training with respect to various service-learning models appropriate to their disciplines, as well as administrative support in organizing and coordinating activities with service site personnel. Indeed, the major reason provided by faculty who do not teach service-learning courses was that they were not sure how the service-learning process worked. Specifically, they needed training in what content areas were appropriate, how to develop site contacts, how to balance the required curriculum with experiential learning, and the general details of how much time students spend at the site, assignments, and course requirements.

Comparisons between faculty and students on their perceptions of the outcomes of service-learning experiences resulted in an interesting pattern. Faculty rated service-learning outcomes more favorably than did students. However, when students were grouped into those who had and had not participated in service-learning, results showed that faculty and service-learning students, relative to nonservice-learning students, believed that students who had participated in service-learning had a better understanding of societal problems and richer educational experiences, were better problems solvers, more compassionate, and more sensitive than students who had not participated in service-learning. The differences in perceptions between service-learning and nonservice-learning students could be a function of the need of service-learning students to justify the time and effort they expended beyond normal course work in the service-learning section of the course they took. Clearly, however, no similar explanation would be plausible for the perception on the part of the majority of faculty of the positive outcomes provided by a service-learning experience, since the majority of faculty have not offered service-learning courses.

The results of this study are noteworthy and clearly reflect the importance of service-learning. Some learning outcomes cannot be transfused into a passive student sitting in a lecture hall, but must involve some form of "real world" experience, the kind that service-learning experiences may offer. The present study suggests that faculty and students who have participated in service-learning believed this opportunity can be an important and valuable learning process which promotes care, compassion, and understanding of societal issues and inequities. It should be noted, however, that this research was conducted at a small, private, metropolitan, Jesuit University with a mission that includes life long learning and commitment to community service. These results may have been different had the study been done at a large public University or College.

While the benefits of service-learning are quite lucid, there are some serious challenges for colleges and universities interested in offering service-learning programs to their students. First, it should be noted that not all faculty supported the concept of service-learning. When faculty were grouped into academic divisions (humanities, social sciences, natural sciences, and business), faculty in the humanities and social sciences more frequently showed an interest in offering service-learning courses on a regular basis. Second, some students view service-learning as just another hoop through which they must jump to complete their academic degree requirements. For this reason, service-learning should be offered as an option rather than a requirement. Third, the academic administration must support service-learning and provide assistance with administrative needs of those working with service sites. In summary, the most successful service-learning programs are those in which there is a natural fit between the mission of the institution, academic course work, faculty expertise, and student interests. Future research should continue on service-learning and focus upon the role faculty play in the success of these programs as well as student achievement and outcomes.

REFERENCES

Ansbaucher, H. L. (1968). The concept of social interest. *Journal of Individual Psychology, 23,* 131-149.

Astin, A. W. (1984). Student involvement: A developmental theory for higher education. *Journal of College Student Development, 25,* 297-308.

Astin, A. W. (1990). *The American freshman: National norms for fall 1990.* Los Angeles: American Council on Education and University of California at Los Angeles.

Clary, E. G., Synder, M., Ridge, R. D., Miene, P. K., & Haugen, J. A. (1994). Matching messages to motives in persuasion: A functional approach to promoting volunteerism. *Journal of Applied Social Psychology, 32,* 50-54.

Costa, P. T. Jr., & VandenBos, G. R. (Eds.). (1990). *Psychological aspects of serious illness: Chronic conditions, fatal diseases, and clinical care.* Washington, DC: American Psychological Association.

Crowner, D. (1995). Semester break service-learning: A two-week off-campus immersion program. *Service-learning: Linking academic and the community.* Harrisburg, PA: Pennsylvania Campus Contact.

Eby, J. W. (1995). Service-learning as scholarship. *Service-learning: Linking academic and the community.* Harrisburg, PA: Pennsylvania Campus Contact.

Edlin, G., Golanty, E., & McCormack Brown, K. (1997). *Essentials for health and wellness.* Sudbury, MA: Jones and Bartlett.

Fitch, R. T. (1991). Differences among community service volunteers, extracurricular volunteers, and nonvolunteers on the college campus. *Journal of College Student Development, 32,* 534-540.

Herek, G. M., & Glunt, E. K. (1988). An epidemic of stigma: Public reactions to AIDS. *American Psychologist, 43,* 886-891.

Hettman, D. W. & Jenkins, E. (1990). Volunteerism and social interest. *Journal of Individual Psychology, 46,* 298-303.

Huwar, B. W. (1995). Partnerships in education project: Learning and service together for all children. *Service-learning: Linking academic and the community.* Harrisburg, PA: Pennsylvania Campus Contact.

Independent Sector. (1981). *Americans Volunteer.* Washington, DC: Author.

Independent Sector. (1988). *Giving and volunteering in the United States: Findings from a national survey.* Washington, DC: Author.

Independent Sector (1992). *Giving and volunteering in the United States: Findings from a national survey.* Washington, DC: Author.

Long, E. (1995). A rhetorical approach for assessing mentor's literacy learning. *Service-learning: Linking academic and the community.* Harrisburg, PA: Pennsylvania Campus Contact.

Marlatt, G. A., & Gordon, J. R. (Eds.) (1985). *Relapse prevention: Maintenance strategies in addictive behavior change.* New York: Guilford.

Miller, T. K., & Prince, J. S. (1976). *The future of student affairs: A guide to student development for tomorrow's higher education.* San Francisco: Jossey-Bass.

Palestini, R. H., Rowe, M. M., & Chapman, J. G. (1997). Service-learning and the carative treatment model. *Journal of Continuing Higher Education, 45(2),* 34-38.

Rosenberg, C. E. (1987). *The cholera years: The United States in 1832, 1849, 1866 (2nd Ed.).* Chicago: University of Chicago Press.

Rowe, M. M., Palestini, R. H., & Chapman, J. G. (1997). Incorporation of community-based service-learning into university curriculum. *Higher Education Abstracts, 32(2),* 135.

Serow, R. C. (1991). Students and volunteerism: Looking into the motives of community service participants. *American Educational Research Journal, 28,* 543-556.

Serow, R. C., Ciechalski, J., & Daye, C. (1990). Students as volunteers: Personal competence, social diversity, and community service. *Urban Education, 25,* 157-168.

Sharon, N. (1991). Fitting volunteers with tasks and creating tasks for volunteers: A look at the role of volunteers in a community context. *Journal of Volunteer Administration, 5,* 4-12.

Vaidya, S. R., & Clark, S. (1995). Promoting critical thinking through academic service learning: A cognitive and affective model for learning how to learn. *Service-Learning: Linking Academic and the Community.* Harrisburg, PA: Pennsylvania Campus Contact.

Ward, C. R., & McCrea, J. M. (1995), Evaluation of a collaborative intergenerational community service project. *Service-Learning: Linking Academic and the Community.* Harrisburg, PA: Pennsylvania Campus Contact.

Attitudinal and Academic Effects of Service-Learning

Elizabeth B. Gardner
Corinne M. Baron

Fairfield University

SUMMARY. We examined perceived learning and attitude change in classes in Cognitive Psychology and Sensation and Perception in which some but not all of the students did service-learning with autistic children or in other settings. Attitudes toward people served became more positive based on questionnaire and journal entry data, and in one class, service-learning students felt they learned more about course material from their experiences. *[Article copies available for a fee from The Haworth Document Delivery Service: 1-800-342-9678. E-mail address: getinfo@haworth pressinc.com]*

Service-learning, which overlaps experiential learning, community-based learning, experiential diversity education, and other kinds of learning, is growing in popularity in American education. A useful definition (T. Stanton, quoted in Cohen & Kinsey, 1994) is that service-learning is "a particular form of experiential education, one that emphasizes for students the accomplishment of tasks which meet human needs in combination with conscious

---

Address correspondence to: Dr. Elizabeth B. Gardner, Department of Psychology-BNW, Fairfield University, Fairfield, CT 06430 (E-mail: gardner@fair1.fair field.edu).

The authors wish to thank Susan Rakowitz for her many helpful suggestions and comments on the manuscript.

[Haworth co-indexing entry note]: "Attitudinal and Academic Effects of Service-Learning." Gardner, Elizabeth B., and Corinne M. Baron. Co-published simultaneously in *Journal of Prevention & Intervention in the Community* (The Haworth Press, Inc.) Vol. 18, No. 1/2, 1999, pp. 97-109; and: *Educating Students to Make-a-Difference: Community-Based Service Learning* (ed: Joseph R. Ferrari, and Judith G. Chapman) The Haworth Press, Inc., 1999, pp. 97-109. Single or multiple copies of this article are available for a fee from The Haworth Document Delivery Service [1-800-342-9678, 9:00 a.m. - 5:00 p.m. (EST). E-mail address: getinfo@haworthpressinc.com].

educational growth" (pp. 5-6). In fact, at the college level, workshops on service-learning are frequent, journals are appearing (e.g., *Michigan Journal of Community Service-Learning*), service-learning electronic "bulletin boards" are emerging, and service-learning Web pages are developing. Some universities have offices specifically created to facilitate service-learning.

Recently, President Clinton proclaimed, "Commitment to community should be an ethic that our children learn as early as possible, so that they carry it with them throughout their lives. That is why I have called on every state to make service a part of the curriculum in high school or even middle school" (radio address, 7/26/97). Some theorists disagree with this view, taking the position that education should be strictly academic, not social or political (Finn, 1995). Others take a very different position: that a mission of a university IS to solve community problems (Brackley, 1992; Harkavy, 1996). Zlotkowski (1996) offers a pragmatic consideration: If service-learning is to become a lasting component in American education, it must have a clear link to "the academy." Advocates must focus on enhanced learning, in his view, with development of moral and civic values and benefits to the community seen as positive but secondary results.

Service-learning is being evaluated extensively at the middle- and high school level as part of Learn and Serve America, a federally-funded program. An interim report (1997) suggests, "Well-designed service-learning programs can strengthen civic attitudes, promote volunteer activity, and improve learning in young people. . . . "

At the college level, there has not been a great deal of evaluation of service-learning. Two studies of the academic value of service-learning have used students' Likert-type ratings of agreement with statements. Markus, Howard, and King (1993) compared data from students enrolled in course sections who were randomly assigned to do service-learning and those who were not assigned. Markus et al.'s (1993) service-learning students did 20 hours of service in one of various community agencies, discussed their experiences in section meetings, and wrote a short paper at the end of the course. Students indicated their agreement with statements such as "I learned to apply principles from this course to new situations"; "I developed a greater awareness of societal problems"; "I reconsidered many of my former attitudes"; "I developed a greater sense of personal responsibility"; and "I feel that I am performing up to my potential in this course" (p. 415). Results indicated a statistically significant difference between the profiles of means on . . . eight items . . . for students in the traditional versus service-learning sections . . . " (p. 414). Markus et al. (1993) reported a difference in final grades, but Miller (1994) claimed that drawing conclusions from service-learners' final grades is complicated by differing course requirements and the possibility that the service-learners' assignments were graded more leniently.

In Miller's (1994) study, students had the option of enrolling in a community service learning course, Project Outreach, in which they did 40 hours of service work, wrote journals, attended classes, and wrote a final paper. Miller (1994) reported that developmental psychology students who did service agreed significantly more with the statements "I learned to apply principles from this course to new situations" and "I developed the ability to solve real problems in this field" than students who did not do service-learning. However, he did not find greater agreement with "I gained a good understanding of concepts in this field" or "I learned about social factors that influence people's development," nor was there a difference in final grades.

By administering questionnaires at both the beginning and end of the semester, both Markus et al. (1993) and Miller (1994) established the clear expectation that the service-learning experience would affect the students' learning and performance in the course. This introduced the possibility that any rating differences between groups might be due to demand characteristics. Service-learners may have felt they were "supposed to" agree with statements like, "I learned to apply principles from this course to new situations." We avoided this problem by asking all students at the end of the course to rate how much they had learned on various topics.

We were also interested in our students' attitudes toward the recipients of their service. Theorists speak of the educational value of "subvert(ing) the dissociation process (of distancing ourselves from homeless people)" (Saltzman and Curtis, 1994) and of helping students "to experience the life of the poor—and reflect on that experience" (Brackley, 1992). Earlier, we had developed a seminar on homelessness and included a service-learning component: in addition to doing readings, watching videotapes, having discussions, and working on an individual project, students spent three hours per week in various sites including soup kitchens and shelters, then reflected on these experiences by keeping journals and writing reflection papers. In order to evaluate the effectiveness of this seminar in changing students' attitudes toward people who were homeless, students were asked to fill out a questionnaire at the beginning of the course and again at the end. We used Guzewicz and Takooshian's (1992) Survey on Social Issues, which includes five statements assessing People's Attitudes Toward Homelessness [PATH]. We intermixed items from the Crowne-Marlow Social Desirability Scale to assess the likelihood of students' answering in response to perceived demand characteristics. Seminar students' scores on the PATH scale changed significantly in the direction of becoming more "humanitarian" as the course progressed. Social Desirability scores did not change significantly; therefore the change in the PATH score of the seminar group could not be attributed to their having given more "socially desirable" responses in response to demand characteristics (Gardner, MacAvoy, & Carrier, 1996). All of the seminar students had done service-learning, however. In order to test the effect of service-learning on student attitudes toward the people served, we would need to integrate service-learning into a course in which some students did service-learning and some did not.

We examined attitudinal and academic effects of service-learning. Rather than asking very general questions about learning which seem particularly susceptible to the influence of demand characteristics, we decided to assess students' perception of their learning of specific aspects of course content. We were careful not to draw attention to the existence of two different groups, and we gave the same questionnaire to all students at the end of the course only. Our prediction was that service-learners would report higher levels of perceived learning than non-service-learners, particularly on the topic of individual differences in cognitive processes, since each placement exposed service-learning students to people "different" from themselves in terms of cognition.

In Study 1 we qualitatively assessed service-learners' attitudes toward people served by counting themes in journal entries; in Study 2, we used a short questionnaire in an attempt to measure change in service-learners' attitude toward autistic children. Our prediction was that there would be a "subversion of the dissociation" between students and the people served.

STUDY 1

Students were randomly assigned to a Service-Learning (S-L) or Non-Service-Learning (N) group in each of two sections of a Cognitive Psychology course. We tested the hypothesis that service-learning enhances academic learning. We assessed students' attitudes by content analyzing reflective passages from their weekly journal entries into themes.

METHOD

Participants

Of 50 students, 21 (7 males, 14 females) were randomly chosen to do service-learning. An additional seven students (all female) who were not picked initially asked to participate, bringing the total to 28 students doing service-learning. Twenty-two students (10 male, 12 female) did not participate in service learning. Students, aged 19-22, were predominantly upper-level Psychology majors, Caucasian, middle- to upper-middle class, and Catholic.

Measures

A questionnaire was constructed with the goal of assessing perceived academic learning while minimizing or eliminating demand characteristics. We presented questions about academic learning on the front page of our questionnaire. We did not ask students to indicate whether they had or had not done service-learning. (Students provided their ID number, used throughout the course, from which we could later decode who was in each group.) Specifically, we asked each student to rate (on a six-point scale) his or her knowledge of Attention, Memory, Language, Cognitive Development, Metacognition, Individual Differences in cognitive processes, and Thinking. Each topic had the numbers 1-6 or 6-1 typed beneath it, with end points labelled as "very well" (6) and "not at all well" (1). Subsequent pages asked general questions about the course, etc. The questionnaire was given to each student at the end of the course.

Procedures

We announced that we would have a lottery to see which students would do service-learning as part of the Cognitive Psychology course. Although we had been concerned that students would be resistant to this idea, they accepted it readily. Two students dropped the course, not necessarily because of service-learning. One remaining student was adamant that she did not have the time for service-learning; she was excused from it. Students who were chosen for service-learning as well as the seven who had asked to participate spent two hours each week in their placement (ideally; some missed some weeks).

Sites were chosen on the basis of relevance to the class material. Student preferences were solicited and then students were assigned to sites, which included: Giant Steps (a program for autistic and learning-disabled children), Best Buddies (which pairs students with mentally-handicapped people), and Head Start, which places students as helpers in classrooms in inner-city Bridgeport, CT. Service-learning students were to hand in copies of their journals weekly. Reflection was stressed in the journal guidelines printed in the syllabus.

The questionnaire was handed out on the last day of class as part of the feedback solicited for the course. Students were assured that their responses would not be examined individually but that they would be pooled for analysis after all grades had been computed.

Students doing service-learning kept journals, copies of which they submitted weekly. Each reflective passage was photocopied for content analysis by the instructor at the end of the course. Consistent themes emerged from the passages. Frequency of each theme was counted.

RESULTS

We hypothesized that service-learning would enhance academic learning. This hypothesis was tested by comparing scores of those students doing service-learning (S-L) and those not service-learning (N) on their rating of knowledge of seven areas of course content. Service-learners reported greater knowledge in only one academic area, Cognitive Development ($F(1,48)$ = 2.11, p = .04; Table 1). Service-learners reported knowledge of Individual Differences was not significantly greater than that of non-service-learners ($t[48]$ = 1.13, p>.05). Final grades in the course did not differ ($t[48]$ = .13, p >.05). It should be noted, however, that seven students had self-selected into service-learning. If their scores were deleted, the Cognitive Development difference no longer reached significance.

Many passages from journals indicated learning and changes in students' attitudes toward the recipients of service-learning. The tally of themes is shown in Table 2. "I can learn from 'them'" and "'they' are unfairly discriminated against" were the two most frequent, with "'they' are like me"

TABLE 1. Ratings of Knowledge of Course Material

Topic	S-L *M* n = 28	S-L *SD*	N *M* n = 22	N *SD*
Attention	4.96	.74	4.96	.49
Memory	4.89	.83	5.05	.65
Language	4.64	.87	4.46	.74
Cognitive Dev.	5.04	.69	4.59	.80
Metacognition	4.36	.83	4.59	1.01
Individual Diffs.	4.86	.65	4.59	1.01
Thinking	4.68	.72	4.46	.74

TABLE 2. Frequency of Themes from 55 Reflective Passages in Cognitive Psychology Students' Journals

This has changed the way think – 3
I see the world through their eyes – 4
It's not their fault – 3
They are like me – 9
I can learn from them – 13
They are unfairly discriminated against – 10
I am learning about diversity and a world wider than my own – 9
I can make a difference – 7

and "I am learning about diversity and a world wider than my own" closely following. Presumably the themes mirrored changing attitudes of service-learning students. An example of a journal entry is the following:

> When I first found out that I was chosen for the service-learning component of the course, I thought to myself, 'Wow, this is great; just one more thing that I have to do.' Looking back now on those feelings I think to myself how lucky I am to have found such a wonderful friend in someone who I probably would have never met otherwise.
>
> I was very nervous when I first met my Best Buddy. His spirit for life and his will to survive made me realize that handicapped people are no different than any other "normal" person. He welcomed me completely and befriended me like no one else I have ever met. I look forward to our daily conversations because unlike many of the conversations that we encounter I know that the person on the other end of the line is actually listening and caring about what I am saying. He and I have conversations like no other that I have ever had before. After our telephone conversation is over I think to myself about all of the discrimination that he must receive because of nothing more than a handicap. If only people would take the time to listen and learn from challenged people they will learn things about themselves and feel things that they never thought that they would feel. Why do we as a society confine these people more than they already are? We confine them through the simple act of discrimination whether it be in direct contact or through indirect contact (jokes, etc.). Since I have become involved in Best Buddies I have truly grown more sensitive to issues that regard people. I attempt to place myself in the role of a physically or mentally handicapped person and attempt to feel how they are feeling. When a situation arises now where a comment or joke is made I stand up for my beliefs because I feel as though I am standing up not only for myself but also for my Best Buddy. (J.S., 10/21/96)

(Three themes were counted in this entry: "They" are just like me, "they" are unfairly discriminated against, and I can learn from "them.")

DISCUSSION

Service-learners reported perceptions of greater academic learning in one of seven specific aspects of course material, Cognitive Development. This is not surprising. Developmental differences from the students characterized the clients in all of the service-learning settings. We had hypothesized that they would report more understanding of individual differences in cognition, but such was not the case. Final grades did not differ between service-learners and non-service-learners.

Students' attitudes toward the people served in service-learning appeared to show change during the semester. Although there was no comparison group and the assessment was non-objective, there seemed to be an increased appreciation for diversity, and a new understanding that one can learn from "the other." We attribute the change in our students' attitudes to the breaking down of "the other" stereotype accomplished during service-learning. As one student observed, "you have to get to know people before you can change your attitude toward them." Indeed, it was striking that the theme which appeared most often in the cognitive psychology students' journals was "I can learn from 'them.'" Gibboney (1996) also reported that service-learners ". . . develop(ed) a respect for "otherness" and reject(ed) stereotypes."

Although it seemed from reading student journals that there had been attitude change, there was the possibility of experimenter bias, and it was felt that a questionnaire would provide more objective data. In a Sensation and Perception course we had an opportunity to compare attitudes toward people who are autistic between a service-learning group and an "equally-motivated" control group. Since only one of seven measures of perceived learning had shown a difference between groups in Study 1, it was decided to investigate perceived learning as well in the Sensation and Perception class.

STUDY 2

Service-learning was added to a course in Sensation and Perception on an optional basis. It was felt that autism was a relevant topic for this class, so only the program for autistic children was used as a service-learning site.

Participants

Of 57 students in two sections of the course, only 16 opted to do service-learning. Because of scheduling difficulties with the program for autistic children, only 10 of those students could be accommodated. This created an "equally motivated" control group (N = 6) against which the service-learning group (N = 10) could be compared in attitude toward autistic people and rating of learning of course material.

Materials

An attitude questionnaire was constructed by modifying that used earlier in the seminar on homelessness (Guzewicz and Takooshian's [1992] Survey on Social Issues, including five statements called the PATH scale (People's Attitudes Toward Homelessness), intermixed with items from the Crowne-Marlow Social Desirability Scale). Only three of the statements in the PATH scale seemed appropriate for use, so these were adapted (changing "homeless" to "autistic") and interspersed with five items from the Social Desirability scale. The three statements then read:

> "Though I know that their condition is not their own fault, I find autistic people unpleasant to be around;" "Kindness, generosity, and love are characteristics found more among autistic people than among non-autistic people;" and "Society is turning away and letting down autistic people." A "Feedback Questionnaire" was also given to each student, who was asked to rate how well they thought they knew the course material (titles of chapters from the textbook were listed). The format was the same as that used in Study 1.

Service-learning students submitted journals weekly. Because the focus was on objective evaluation of attitudes, however, no formal content analysis was performed.

Procedures

The resulting short attitude questionnaire and the Feedback Questionnaire were given to all 57 students at the end of the course. To encourage honesty, no identifying numbers were used. After all the questionnaires were completed, questionnaires from students in the equally-motivated control group were collected individually and put into an envelope. The rest of the students were asked to put their questionnaires into the Service-Learning envelope or the Non-Service-Learning envelope, depending on whether or not they had done service-learning. Thus we could look at attitudes toward autistic people and perceived mastery of course material in those students who had done service-learning and those equally-motivated students who had not.

Results

There was a difference in attitude toward people who are autistic between service-learners and the equally-motivated control group. Service-learners disagreed more strongly than did equally-motivated controls with "though I know that their condition is not their own fault, I find autistic people unpleasant to be around" (t (12) = 3.96, p < .002). There was also a significant difference on "Society is turning away and letting down autistic people" (t (13) = 3.13, p = .008). Scores did not differ on "Kindness, generosity, and love are characteristics found more among autistic people than among non-

TABLE 3. Attitude Questions, Social Desirability Questions, and Knowledge of Material

Question	S-L *M* n = 10	S-L *SD*	Eq. Motiv. *M* n = 6	Eq. Motiv. *SD*
Not Their Fault	5.90	.32	4.60	.90
More Kind, etc.	3.60	1.26	3.20	.84
Society	3.30	.95	4.83	.98
Social Desirability	4.46	1.36	4.50	1.43
Course Material	4.75	.84	4.95	.65

autistic people" (t [12] = .39, p > .05; see Table 3). There was no difference in the scores on the Social Desirability questions (t [78] =.13, p > .05). Grouping all 10 chapters together, the two groups did not differ in perceived mastery of course material (t[158] = 1.58, p > 05).

Discussion

The difference in attitude toward people who are autistic between service-learners and equally-motivated controls was striking. Students who had done service-learning strongly disagreed with the assertion that people who are autistic are unpleasant to be around. This question most clearly reflected a more positive attitude toward autistic people on the part of service-learners. The second question, "Kindness, generosity and love are characteristics found more among autistic people than among non-autistic people," may simply have been recognized as vapid by both groups. Service-learners agreed less than equally-motivated controls with the third question, "Society is turning away and letting down autistic people," probably because service-learners were spending time each week in a program in which a number of people were working very actively to teach autistic children and integrate them into local schools.

That there was no difference in perceived mastery of course material was not entirely surprising, given that autism was not specifically covered as a course topic. Although journal entries were not formally scored, at least some service-learning students seemed to have gained an enriched appreciation of the broader field and greater understanding of the difficulty in explaining even normal perception, much less why one child was said to feel as though he were in a wetsuit, and why another found eating crackers excruciatingly painful.

GENERAL DISCUSSION

The recently-released (1997) interim report of the federally-funded program "Learn and Serve America" cites increased learning at the middle- and high school level as one of the benefits of service-learning. College-level service-learners in the studies of Markus et al. (1993) and Miller (1994) agreed more strongly with "I learned to apply principles from this course to new situations" than did controls. Cohen and Kinsey (1994) reported that "the greatest strength of the community projects appears to be in helping university students to place classroom material into a meaningful context" (p. 8), and that ". . . service learning is more than *doing good*. It is an effective means of teaching that increases student understanding of complex material" (p. 13). The present study (Study 1) provided evidence of students' perception of enhanced knowledge of specific course material at the college level. It is clear that service-learning does not produce a strong, across-the-board magnification of knowledge of course material, however. Service-learners' and non-service-learners' final grades did not differ, and a comparison of service-learners' and non-service-learners' test scores in a subsequent semester of Cognitive Psychology yielded a trend in the expected direction but failed to reach significance.

If we were to ask very specific questions (e.g., "How much do you know about autism?"), we might find differences between service-learners and controls, but would that be of value? Very specific questions are open to the criticism that student service-learners, if answering differently, are responding to demand characteristics–the expectation that they should know a lot about autism. There is also the criticism that service-learners, who inevitably put in more time as a result of service-learning than students who do not, may experience a cognitive dissonance effect: "if I spent this much time for this course, it must have been of benefit to me." Given these considerations, it is difficult to unassailably demonstrate enhanced academic learning from service-learning, even if such be the case.

Markus et al. (1993) suggest that service-learning extends academic learning. It exposes students to worlds that otherwise they might not know exist. Is this not what higher education is about? Brackley (1992) writes

> The university does not fulfill its function today unless it allows its students to break out of their narrow world, to broaden their horizons and formulate the questions they really need for a university education worthy of the name. . . . Far from distracting students from studies, this experience stimulates the kinds of profound questions, courses and term papers that represent real education. (p. 13)

Measuring attitudinal change appears to be a useful approach. In the Markus et al. (1993) study,

> students in the service-learning sections . . . provided higher mean ratings of the degree to which they thought that participation in the

course had increased or strengthened their "intention to serve others in need," "intention to give to charity," "orientation toward others and away from yourself," "belief that helping those in need is one's social responsibility," "belief that one can make a difference in the world," and "tolerance and appreciation of others. . ." (p. 413)

Miller (1994) reported that students in the service-learning sections agreed significantly more than students in traditional sections with "I reconsidered many of my former attitudes" and "I developed a greater sense of personal responsibility" (p. 415).

To be sure, enhanced learning of course material is important, but our experience with service-learning has caused us to broaden our idea of learning and of what is important for students to learn. When students in the Cognitive Psychology course wrote on the theme of learning from "the other," they did not mean learning about course material as much as about life, people, and values. Miller (1994) says:

> traditional in-class graded assignments and tests do not generally tap what successful community service learning experiences seem most positively to affect: *first-hand knowledge of the real world* (emphasis added), abilities in areas directly related to the field experience, and capacities for applying concepts to the world outside of the classroom. (p. 34)

Students clearly think the experience is valuable. In our Seminar on Homelessness we asked students what percentage of what they had learned about homelessness was from service-learning. Responses indicated that more than a third of their learning, twice as much as from any other course component, had been from service-learning. Even in more traditionally academic courses such as Cognitive Psychology and Sensation and Perception, students felt they learned a great deal from service-learning. For example, a Cognitive Psychology student wrote,

> I remember the day in class when I volunteered to pick the names for the service learning component. I was just trying to be helpful but to be honest, I wasn't really awake yet and did not even know what I was doing. Anyway, I ended up choosing my own name and was not happy about it. At that time I was overwhelmed because I'm a senior, my classes had a tough work load, I was applying for a Fulbright grant and on top of all of this my family life was a mess. I am a firm believer in fate, that everything happens for a reason. I am so grateful that I was picked to do the service learning component because it turned out to be one of the greatest experiences of my life. P. S., 11/24/97

This is strong affirmation. We subscribe to the ideal that students will serve, reflect on that experience, educate others, and ultimately advocate for the people they have served. Attitudinal change and real-world knowledge acquired from service-learning seem at least as important as enhanced academic learning.

REFERENCES

Brackley, D. (1992). The Christian university and liberation: The challenge of the UCA. *Discovery: Jesuit International Ministries.* St. Louis, MO: The Institute of Jesuit Sources.

Cohen, J. and Kinsey, D. (1994). "Doing good" and scholarship: A service-learning study. *Journalism Educator*, Winter, 4-14.

Finn, C. E., Jr. and Vanourek, G. (1995). Charity begins at school. (Critique of service learning.) *Commentary*, 100, 46-48.

Gardner, E. B., MacAvoy, S. and Carrier, P. E. (1996, March). Attitudes toward homeless people changed by seminar. Paper presented at the meeting of the Eastern Psychological Association, Philadelphia, PA.

Gibboney, R. (1996). Service-learning and commitment to community: Exploring the implications of honors students' perceptions of the process 2 years later. *Nonprofit and Voluntary Sector Quarterly, 25,* 506-524.

Guzewicz, T. D. and Takooshian, H. (1992). Development of a short-form scale of public attitudes toward homelessness. *Journal of Social Distress and the Homeless 1,* 67-79.

Harkavy, I. (1996). Service learning workshop. Presented at the University of Hartford, Hartford, CT.

Learn and Serve America Office. (1997). Learn and Serve America Interim Report. (BRoberts@cns.gov).

Markus, G. B., Howard, J. P. F. and King, D. C. (1993). Integrating community service and classroom instruction enhances learning: Results from an experiment. *Educational Evaluation and Policy Analysis 15,* 410-419.

Miller, J. (1994). Linking traditional and service-learning courses: Outcome evaluations using two pedagogically distinct models. *Michigan Journal of Community Service Learning 1,* 29-36.

Saltzman, A. L. and Curtis, F. (1994). Social distress theory and teaching about homelessness: A retrospective analysis. *Journal of Social Distress and the Homeless 3,* 99-133.

Zlotkowski, E. (1996). Linking service-learning and the academy. *Change,* Jan./Feb., 21-27.

Student Perceptions of the "Learning" in Service-Learning Courses

Maria W. McKenna
Elaine Rizzo

Saint Anselm College

SUMMARY. The purpose of this study was to examine perceptions of student impact of service learning on academic, personal, and civic development. All participants (n = 202) submitted journals and completed questionnaires which contained a combination of categorical and Likert-type items and open-ended questions. The study was conducted over a period of three semesters. Students reported perceiving a positive impact of service learning on understanding of course concepts and class learning, increased understanding of and ability to relate to differences in others, increased self-awareness and self-confidence, and increased appreciation for and commitment to service. Student perceptions were examined using ANOVA and non-parametric tests. Test results were supplemented with student journal entries. Results support the positive outcomes on student academic, personal, and social development reported in service learning literature. *[Article copies available for a fee from The Haworth Document Delivery Service: 1-800-342-9678. E-mail address: getinfo@haworthpressinc.com]*

Recent studies of service learning have begun to demonstrate the value of community service in facilitating the understanding of course material, as

---

Address correspondence to: Maria W. McKenna, Department of Psychology, Saint Anselm College, 100 Saint Anselm Drive, Manchester, NH 03102-1310 (E-mail: mmckenna@anselm.edu).

The authors wish to thank Dan Forbes and the student coordinators at the Saint Anselm College Center For Volunteers for their assistance.

[Haworth co-indexing entry note]: "Student Perceptions of the "Learning" in Service Learning Courses." McKenna, Maria W., and Elaine Rizzo. Co-published simultaneously in *Journal of Prevention & Intervention in the Community* (The Haworth Press, Inc.) Vol. 18, No. 1/2, 1999, pp. 111-123; and: *Educating Students to Make-a-Difference: Community-Based Service Learning* (ed: Joseph R. Ferrari, and Judith G. Chapman) The Haworth Press, Inc., 1999, pp. 111-123. Single or multiple copies of this article are available for a fee from The Haworth Document Delivery Service [1-800-342-9678, 9:00 a.m. - 5:00 p.m. (EST). E-mail address: getinfo@haworthpressinc.com].

111

well as helping students achieve other personal and educational goals (McCluskey-Fawcett & Grefen, 1992) and stimulating student interest in course material and related issues (Glenwick & Chabot, 1991). Markus, Howard and King (1993) found that classroom learning and course grades increased significantly as a result of students' participation in course-relevant community service. Kendrick (1996) showed that students in a service learning section of Introductory Sociology improved on several indicators, such as social responsibility and indicators of personal efficacy (a belief that one can make a difference in the world). Kuh (1993) found that experiences beyond the classroom, such as community-based service made substantial contributions to student learning and personal development. In that study, all students reported meaningful changes in their interpersonal and practical competencies and critical thinking abilities. Kuh points out that experiences outside the classroom may be important venues where students develop an appreciation for people from diverse backgrounds and cultivate skills which enable them to relate personally to others.

Not all studies of the outcome of service learning experiences, however, have produced identical results. Hudson (1996) measured changes in student attitudes and values after completing a service learning component of a public policy course. Analysis of pre and post-test results failed to demonstrate significant impact of service learning on students' prosocial and civic attitudes. Miller (1994) examined students in two advanced introductory psychology courses, some of whom selected an option for community service learning. Interestingly, students in the two courses (service learning versus non-service-learning) did *not* differ in their reports concerning gains in personal development, general mastery of course concepts, or in their final course grades received. However, participants did report an enhanced ability to apply concepts outside the classroom, which is consistent with results from other studies (Blankenship and McGowan, 1994; Gardner, 1997; Kuh, 1993; Kupiec, 1993; Myers-Lipton, 1996). Miller noted that helping students to be able to successfully apply knowledge learned in the classroom to the real world, as well as acquire discipline-based concepts evaluated by traditional exams, are basic and critical goals of education and are of particular importance within higher education. Similar results were demonstrated by Batchelder and Root (1994), who found that service-learning participants made greater gains than students in traditional classes on several dimensions of thinking about social problems, such as multidimensionality (the number of dimensions of a situation considered when responding to hypothetical problem situations) and uncertainty/resolve (a resolve to act despite explicitly acknowledged uncertainty of the success of the action). Service learning, according to these authors, influenced participants' use of prosocial decision making and resulted in both a greater resolve to act in the face of acknowledged uncertainty and an enhanced awareness of the uncertainty involved when dealing with social problems.

As service learning becomes more widely established on college campuses across the country, faculty and administrators are keenly interested in outcomes assessment and evidence of the impact of service-learning experiences. Despite the growing body of literature on service learning, there remains a need for further studies that examine its impact on students. Previous research has examined the effects of service learning in three primary domains–academic, personal, and social responsibility. The present study also focused on the impact of service learning in these three areas but differed from prior studies in several ways. Unlike much of the literature which examined service learning over a one-semester individual course or service learning sections of a course, this study examined students enrolled in 17 different courses across six disciplines over a three semester time period. Additionally, much of the literature has focused on service learning effects with little comparative analysis of student outcomes based on student major, type of service site, or student expectations and perceptions regarding the impact of service. This study examined these variables and asked students to assess their own perceptions of the influence of their service-learning experiences on their understanding of course concepts, class motivation, personal growth, and attitudes toward community service.

METHOD

Participants

Study participants consisted of 202 male and female undergraduate students enrolled in a small, religious-affiliated, liberal arts college with a student population that is predominantly European-American, middle-class, and Roman Catholic. These demographic characteristics were also reflected in the study participants who represented 11 different majors (Psychology, Criminal Justice, Sociology, Politics, Nursing, Natural Science, Biology, English, History, Business, and Undeclared). Seventy-eight percent of participants were either juniors (47%) or sophomores (31%); 10% were freshmen and 9% were seniors.

Procedure

Students in 17 courses (see Table 1) offered in 6 different disciplines (psychology, criminal justice, sociology, theology, education, and modern languages) were provided with an opportunity to elect a service-learning

TABLE 1. Courses That Offered Service Learning

Psychology

    Physiological Psychology
    Psychology of Adulthood and Aging
    Child Psychopathology
    Child Psychology

Criminal Justice

    Juvenile Justice
    Crisis Intervention
    Victims of Crime and Social Injustice

Sociology

    Social Work I & II
    Social Services
    Medical Sociology

Modern Languages

    Advanced Spanish Grammar
    Culture and Civilization of Latin America

Theology

    Christian Social Ethics

Education

    Introduction to Special Education

assignment as one of several possible course assignments. To fulfill the service-learning option, students were required to volunteer 20 hours of time over the course of the semester, keep written journals of their experiences at the site, and write papers that linked the experiences discussed in the journals with concepts being covered in the course.

The data were obtained over three semesters during 1995 and 1996 from the student journals that were written during each semester and from the questionnaires administered to all service-learning students at the end of each semester. The survey consisted of 21 objective items that asked students about their attitudes toward and expectations for service learning, how their expectations changed, whether they anticipated working with the same client population and issues in the future, and an overall evaluation of their experience; 12 five-point Likert-type (significant positive impact to significant negative impact) items measuring their perceptions of the academic and personal impact of their experiences; and 5 open-ended questions that asked for specific experiences that influenced their responses to the objective items on the survey. The open-ended questions asked students to (a) describe the factors or experiences which contributed to any differences between initial expectations and actual contribution/learning; (b) provide a statement that describes the most significant impact of the service learning experience; (c) what factors motivated the choice of the service learning option; (d) describe one or more incidents, interactions or insights that contributed to any change in motivation; and, (e) evaluate service learning as a teaching method in this course. The return rate was over 90%.

Service Settings

Fifty-six private and non-profit community agencies were used as placement sites. These sites included 15 schools (public and private elementary, middle, and secondary); 18 alternative educational programs, child care facilities, and recreational programs; 4 criminal justice agencies (1 jail, 1 women's prison, 1 juvenile correctional facility, and 1 domestic violence prevention agency); 7 health care facilities and programs (3 nursing homes, 1 adult day care center, 2 public health agencies, and 1 private health care facility); 7 mental health, substance abuse, developmental disabilities and crisis service programs; and 3 poverty and income assistance agencies and programs (2 soup kitchens and 1 low income family service agency). These agencies served a diversified population across several needs categories. Clients ranged in age from infants to elderly, and represented a cross-section of socio-economic, racial, and ethnic groups.

Students provided direct services that included tutoring, mentoring, mediation, conflict resolution, translating, educational and nursing assistance, staffing crisis lines and soup kitchens, child care, geriatric care, recreational activities, leading and facilitating groups, and providing assistance and social support to individuals with Alzheimer's, chronic mental illness, and developmental disabilities.

RESULTS AND DISCUSSION

Academic Impact

When asked "what impact or reinforcement this current service learning had on your understanding of course concepts," 92% of students reported a positive impact ("significant positive"/"moderate positive" impact combined), and 8% reported no impact. Ninety percent responded "yes" to the question "did service learning significantly contribute to learning in class."

When asked how the current service learning experience affected motivation in the course ("significantly increased motivation" to "significantly decreased motivation") 72% reported increased motivation ("significantly increased" and "moderately increased" combined); 27% reported "no change" in motivation, and less than 1% reported a moderate decrease in motivation.

A one-way analysis of variance was conducted to evaluate whether the type of placement site affected students' perceptions of the impact of service learning on understanding of course concepts and motivation in class. No significant differences were found in perceptions of learning or motivation between the six categories of placement sites (criminal justice; poverty and low income assistance; schools; alternative education, recreation, and child care; mental health, substance abuse, crisis services, and developmental disabilities; and health agencies).

The effect of student major on perceptions of how service learning contributed to learning and motivation was examined. Students' majors were collapsed into two categories: social science (psychology, sociology, and criminal justice) and non-social science majors (natural science, biology, history, English, politics, modern languages, business, and nursing). Independent samples *t* tests revealed no significant effect of major on perceptions of service learning impact on academic learning or on motivation in class.

Journals submitted in the psychology and criminal justice courses were examined by the professors in those courses for entries that reflected the students' perceptions of how specific service learning experiences were linked to course concepts. The following examples illustrated students' integration of class concepts with field experiences.

JOURNAL ENTRIES

When we discussed different disorders, I was able to become actively involved in discussions. I would discuss my students. The concepts about the different disorders we studied were brought to life in service learning.

I worked with kids with ADHD, watching them waste a whole class period and get no work done when I know they know the answers. It made me want to learn more about ADHD and why the kids cannot get their work done.

The different levels of cognitive ability of the kids was extremely varied, and I found it challenging to be able to explain the lessons different ways. When the kids finally understood, I was *so* happy.

The state of mind of the clients made me want to learn more about how the mind functions at the cellular level.

After observing the kids, I found myself being more attentive to details that might apply to them from class.

One woman with Alzheimer's Disease responded to me as I was talking to her. She is so far into the disease that it seems she doesn't have any idea what is going on. So this gave me a boost to try and communicate with others, and to pay attention to more facts given about the disease in class.

Personal Impact

One of the most unanticipated outcomes of service learning for students was how much they learned about themselves through the experience of serving others. Students were asked to describe their expectations for service learning and how those expectations changed. As reported in Table 2, one-fourth expected to gain significant learning about others, and 80% expected this learning to be either moderate or significant. In contrast, students were significantly less likely to expect to learn about themselves through service learning ($t(201) = 7.86$, $p < .001$). Also, students expressed nearly 10 times greater uncertainty about how much they will learn about themselves (10%

TABLE 2. Student Ratings of Expected and Actual Learning About Others and Self

	Percent and Number			
Amount of Learning	Expected Learning About Others		Actual Learning About Others	
	%	(n)	%	(n)
Significant	25.2	(51)	55.9	(113)
Moderate	55.4	(112)	33.7	(68)
Slight	18.3	(37)	9.9	(20)
Undecided	1.0	(2)	.5	(1)
	Expected Learning About Self		Actual Learning About Self	
Significant	14.9	(30)	33.7	(68)
Moderate	38.6	(78)	51	(103)
Slight	36.6	(74)	12.4	(25)
Undecided	9.9	(20)	3	(6)

undecided) in comparison to learning about others (1% undecided). Thus, most students entered service learning with higher expectations that they would learn more about others than they would about themselves.

Students did report greater learning about others than about self ($t(201)$ = 5.65, $p < .001$). However, they also learned significantly more about themselves than expected ($t(201)$ = 10.41, $p < .001$). Additionally, students who expected greater self-learning were significantly more likely to perceive greater self-learning than students whose expectations were slight. A Kruskal-Wallis test was conducted to evaluate differences among the three conditions (significant, moderate and slight expectations of learning about self) on actual perceived learning about self. The test was significant, Chi square (2, N = 200) = 45.02, $p < .001$. Follow-up tests were conducted to evaluate pairwise differences among the three groups, using the Holm's sequential Bonferroni approach. The results of these tests indicate that all three pairwise differences were significant. Thus, students who expected more learning about self perceived greater learning about self as a result of service learning. This impact of service learning on self-understanding is further supported in students' comments.

JOURNAL ENTRIES

I learned a great deal about patience, compassion and empowerment. Qualities I rarely think of myself as possessing.

I learned that I could deal with varying types of problems the patients had. It made me realize I could actually be of some aid to my elders. At first, I thought I couldn't work with the elderly, since they're not exactly like children, but I found out that all you have to be is yourself and everything else will fall into place. This gives me more confidence to look within to solve problems and offer help to others.

Today was really an eye-opener because I learned that when you translate for a person you must be aware of the human connection that is going on. I really came to understand myself because I felt what the client must have felt with us there.

Going into [a children's soup kitchen], I had all these visions of helping all these cute little kids; I guess I had a slight case of 'I'll rescue them' fever or something. What I found out from the first minute was that I would be learning more about myself than anyone else.

Through service learning, students not only perceive increased self-understanding, but they also reported greater awareness of their strengths and weaknesses and an increased ability to adapt to challenges and to work with a diverse client population. In the survey, students were asked to evaluate the amount and direction of impact of service learning in these areas with 5-point item responses that ranged from "significant positive impact" to "significant negative impact." After examining inter-item variances, these items (ability to relate to people with different backgrounds or special needs; ability to adapt to challenging situations; awareness of personal strengths or weaknesses; confidence to effectively perform work or service) were combined to form a composite measure of personal growth. The relationship between perceived personal growth and how much students believed they contributed at the service site was examined.

ANOVA and Tukey post hoc comparisons showed that students who perceived making a significant contribution at the site reported significantly greater perceptions of personal growth than students who perceived their site contribution as slight ($F(2,196) = 18.27, p < .001$).

JOURNAL ENTRIES

> I came to realize that the benefits of service are reciprocal . . . [I gained] personal growth and character development. I no longer identify people by their handicap . . . As I began to relate with them I saw real, suffering people, not schizophrenics exhibiting this or that symptom. This growth in understanding improved my self-esteem as I became more aware of the fact that all relationships should be built on respect, knowledge of self and others, and sense of dignity for human life.

> I consider my volunteer work as one of my greatest accomplishments.

> Because I was given so much responsibility, I worked harder to fulfill expectations and take on the responsibility.

Spiritual Dimension of Personal Impact

A more elusive element to assess is the impact that service learning may have on students' spiritual development and faith The survey contained two items that tapped into this dimension of personal growth and development. Students were asked to evaluate the amount and direction of impact of service learning on their beliefs about what is "desirable, important, and good." Eighty-four percent of students perceived service learning as having a positive impact on these beliefs. Only 14% reported no impact and fewer than 1% reported a negative impact. In contrast, when asked about the amount and direction of impact service learning had on their faith, far fewer students (33%) perceived a positive impact. However, 65% of students did not perceive service learning as having any impact, and only 1% reported a negative impact. The spiritual impact of service learning on one student was expressed as follows:

> Although I am not truly affiliated with any denomination, I have realized that there is a spiritual context that contains goodness and good will for all.

Civic Impact and Social Responsibility

The students who choose the service-learning option were required to volunteer 20 hours of time over the course of the semester. However, a substantial number of students (28%) continued to volunteer after their required hours were completed with several (5%) completing between 40 and 70 hours at the placement agencies during the semester. Students' perceptions of their own contributions to the service site were assessed ("significant contribution" to "slight contribution"). Sixty-two percent perceived making a significant contribution, 93% felt they made a moderate contribution, and 44% perceived their contributed as slight. An analysis of variance was computed to test the hypothesis that students who perceived making a greater contribution during service learning would be more likely to report that the service learning experience had made a positive impact on their willingness to engage in community service in the future. The ANOVA was significant, $F(2, 196) = 14.95$, $p < .001$. Post-hoc comparisons using a Tukey test found significant differences between the group that perceived making a "significant" contribution to the placement site and the group that perceived making a "slight" contribution. The group that perceived making a significant contribution reported a greater impact on their aspirations toward future community service.

Numerous student reflections revealed a growing awareness of the important functions that volunteers perform in community agencies and of the personal return that is received through community service.

JOURNAL ENTRIES

> My service learning experience showed me the importance of community service. If people did not volunteer their time, then organizations such as the Salvation Army would not be able to provide services for those who are in need.

You always hear about kids that are poor and hungry but when you actually come face to face with the problem and become closer on a personal level with some of these kids it has an impact on you. You want to help them.

It really opened my eyes to the world. It made me see how many and how important it is that people use their time to help others.

The most significant impact of this experience is simply that experience, be it for volunteering or service learning, is work as much as book learning and through this service learning it has made me more dedicated to getting out in the community.

This 'service learning' idea must have a greater purpose than to put something extraordinary on a resume and to constantly ask what I'm gaining from this experience. Service-learning must, first and foremost, open people's hearts and make them willing to sacrifice their own lives and their own security to help other people in need and, in the process, make the world a better place in which to live.

CONCLUSION

The results reported in this study add to our understanding of the way students perceive their service learning experiences. As has been demonstrated in previous research, most students reported a strong positive impact on academic and personal development. In addition, the present study showed that the impact of service learning is not restricted to certain types of sites, or to certain majors, such as social science students. Instead, students majoring in the humanities or natural sciences perceived similar benefits.

Student expectations of service learning were also addressed in this study. An unanticipated outcome was the amount of unexpected self-learning that resulted from service learning. The finding that students who reported higher expectations of learning from the service experience actually reported greater learning is an important one, and may have implications for the way service learning is presented to students at the beginning of a semester.

Limitations of the present study should be addressed by future research employing longitudinal methods to assess student expectations before beginning service learning, and the relationships of those expectations to outcome measures at the end of the service experience. A problem with the results reported here is that students were asked to report what their expectations had been at the start of the semester, and their reports may have been influenced by the service experience they had just completed.

An additional limitation was the inability of this research to examine the effects of gender on students' perceptions. Gender was intentionally excluded as a demographic variable from the survey because of concerns that it might compromise anonymity due to the small number of males in some courses.

Hedin (1989) points out that learning from service, like any real learning, is highly personal, dependent on both the learning environment and the individual learner. Not all students have powerful learning or personally enriching experiences. However, the voices included in this paper highlighted the power of service learning–its ability to help students integrate theory and practice, and to allow students to become more active participants in the learning process. Additionally, they have provided additional evidence that service learning is a powerful tool for helping students learn how to assess problems and needs and develop solutions within the community.

REFERENCES

Batchelder, T. H., & Root, S. (1994). Effects of an undergraduate program to integrate academic learning and service: Cognitive, prosocial cognitive, and identity outcomes. *Journal of Adolescence, 17*, 341-355.

Gardner. E. B. (1997). *Impact of service-learning on attitudes toward the disadvantaged: Community-based learning about homelessness, aging, and cognition.* Paper presented at the annual meeting of the Eastern Psychological Association, Washington, DC.

Glenwick, D., & Chabot, D. (1991). The undergraduate clinical child psychology course: Bringing students to the real world and the real world to students. *Teaching of Psychology, 18*, 21-24.

Hedin, D. (1989). The power of service. *Proceedings of the Academy of Political Science, 37*, 201-213.

Hedin, D., & Conrad, D. (1987). Community service: A bridge to learning. *Community Education Journal, 15*, 10-14.

Kendrick, J. R. (1996). Outcomes of service-learning in an Introduction to Sociology course. *Michigan Journal of Community Service Learning, 3*, 72-81.

Kuh, G. D. (1993). In their own words: What students learn outside the classroom. *American Education Research Journal, 30*, 277-304.

Markus, G. B., Howard, J. P., & King, D. C. Integrating community service and classroom instruction enhances learning: Results from an experiment. *Educational Evaluation and Policy Analysis, 15*, 410-419.

McCluskey-Fawcett, K., & Green, P. (1992). Using community service to teach developmental psychology. *Teaching of Psychology, 19*, 150-152.

Miller, J. (1994). Linking traditional and service-learning courses: Outcome evaluations utilizing two pedagogically distinct models. *Michigan Journal of Community Service Learning, 1*, 29-36.

Myers-Lipton, S. J. (1996). Effect of a comprehensive service-learning program on college students' level of modern racism. *Michigan Journal of Community Service Learning, 3*, 44-54.

Kupiec, Tamar Y. (1993). *Rethinking tradition: Integrating service with academic study on college campuses.* Providence, RI: Campus Compact Education Commission of the States.

The Unintended Consequences
of Volunteerism:
Positive Outcomes for Those Who Serve

Judy Primavera

Fairfield University

SUMMARY. With over one-half of all college students volunteering for community service activities and increasing numbers of colleges and universities moving towards a greater infusion of service-related learning experiences into the curriculum, it is important to understand the impact volunteerism has on those who serve. This paper presents the results of a qualitative study of the meaning and impact of volunteerism as described by experienced college student volunteers in a Head Start-based Family Literacy Project. Volunteers reported benefits in the areas of self-knowledge, academics, and social awareness. Positive outcomes in the areas of personal growth, self-esteem, and personal efficacy were noted. Service and traditional academics were viewed as mutually enhancing learning strategies; volunteering gave coursework more meaning and what was learned in the classroom increased the volunteers' effectiveness in the community. Increased awareness of impor-

---

Address correspondence to: Judy Primavera, Department of Psychology, Fairfield University, Fairfield, CT 06430 (E-mail: jprimavera@fair1.fairfield.edu).

The author thanks Matthew Cook, Kathleen McGuigan, Anne O'Donnell, and Erica Quinn, for their assistance in data collection and analysis.

This work was supported by the F. M. Kirby Foundation, the Reader's Digest Foundation, Peoples' Bank, Inc., the Corporation for National Service, the College of Arts and Sciences of Fairfield University, and Action for Bridgeport Community Development, Inc.

[Haworth co-indexing entry note]: "The Unintended Consequences of Volunteerism: Positive Outcomes for Those Who Serve." Primavera, Judy. Co-published simultaneously in *Journal of Prevention & Intervention in the Community* (The Haworth Press, Inc.) Vol. 18, No. 1/2, 1999, pp. 125-140; and: *Educating Students to Make-a-Difference: Community-Based Service Learning* (ed: Joseph R. Ferrari, and Judith G. Chapman) The Haworth Press, Inc., 1999, pp. 125-140. Single or multiple copies of this article are available for a fee from The Haworth Document Delivery Service [1-800-342-9678, 9:00 a.m. - 5:00 p.m. (EST). E-mail address: getinfo@haworthpressinc.com].

tant social issues, greater appreciation for diversity, and decreased negative stereotypes were attributed to the volunteer experience. Volunteers also expressed a strong commitment to engaging in some type of community service in the future. Implications for future research are discussed. *[Article copies available for a fee from The Haworth Document Delivery Service: 1-800-342-9678. E-mail address: getinfo@haworthpressinc.com]*

The National and Community Service Acts of 1990 and 1993 motivated America's colleges and universities to focus increased attention on the role of volunteerism in higher education. Universities were being asked to "rethink" their traditional emphasis on teaching and research and to expand their definition of scholarship to include service (Boyer & Hechinger, 1981; Zlotkowski, 1995). Boyer (1994) has called for a "New American College" . . . "an institution that celebrates teaching and selectively supports research, while also taking special pride in its capacity to connect thought to action, theory to practice" (p. A48). According to Boyer, these "new" colleges will create a new model of excellence in higher education, one that will "enrich the campus, renew communities, and give new dignity and status to the scholarship of service" (p. A48). Within this model of education, successful universities of the 21st Century will be those that help to solve our nation's most urgent social problems. Successful graduates of those universities will be individuals who are adept in turning knowledge into productive action. Towards that end, there has been an increasing trend across American colleges and universities to involve students in community service experiences that address important social problems (Deutsch, 1993; Howard, 1993).

Recent discussions of how universities might integrate community volunteer activities into the curricula suggest that such volunteerism should not be viewed solely as "an exercise in altruism" (Markus, Howard & King, 1993). The picture is far more complex than the unidimensional "giver-receiver" stereotype of the "do gooder" college student helping some disenfranchised individual or group. Research confirms that the motivation for volunteering is multi-determined and that volunteerism serves a variety of important functions other than the purely altruistic (Clary, Snyder & Ridge, 1992; Clary, Snyder, Ridge, Copeland, Stukas, Haugen & Miene, 1997). Likewise, recent research on the impact of volunteer activity has expanded the traditional view of "who benefits" from volunteerism. Numerous studies (e.g., Astin, 1993; Batchelder & Root, 1994; Giles & Eyler, 1994) have documented a host of "unintended" positive personal, academic, and social outcomes for those who serve.

Every year, large numbers of college students devote substantial amounts of their time and energy to community service. National surveys suggest that over one-half of all college undergraduates are involved in some type of volunteer activity (Boyer, 1987; Levine, 1994). The combination of both the abundance of college students participating and the number of universities moving towards the infusion of service into their curricula underscores the importance of defining and more fully understanding just "what" constitutes a "successful" volunteer experience. Thus, it is critical that research efforts explore and document the outcomes for student volunteers (Cohen, 1994). The present study represents an important "first step" in the documentation process. It presents a qualitative analysis of how college students with two or more semesters of service in an urban Head Start setting describe the benefits they experienced as a result of volunteering.

METHOD

Participants

During the 1994-1995 and 1995-1996 academic years, 230 undergraduate students at a suburban Northeastern Jesuit university (approximately 3,000 full time undergraduates) volunteered to participate in the Adrienne Kirby Family Literacy Project. Participants served as language tutors for preschool-age children enrolled in an urban Head Start program. To insure that the students' responses reflected a more extensive involvement in community service, only those Family Literacy volunteers with two or more semesters of experience were included in this study. The final sample consisted of 112 "veteran" volunteers, or 49% of the original sample. Volunteers were predominantly female (82%) and White (90%). Their ages ranged from 18 to 22 years old (M = 20 years). Twenty percent were seniors, 41% juniors, 28% sophomores, and 11% freshmen. Volunteers were recruited through announcements posted on campus bulletin boards and by announcements made in psychology and sociology courses.

Volunteer Statistics

Of the 112 volunteers, 46% volunteered for two semesters, 35% for three semesters, and 19% for four semesters. Two semester veterans averaged 34 volunteer hours over 18 separate visits to Head Start; three semester veterans averaged 52 volunteer hours over 27 visits; and four semester veterans averaged 68 volunteer hours over 36 visits. University tutors volunteered an average of 1.9 hours per visit (range 1 to 3 hours) for an aggregate total of over 5,200 volunteer hours over the two-year Project period.

The Adrienne Kirby Family Literacy Project

The Adrienne Kirby Family Literacy Project is a collaborative project between an urban, non-profit family service agency and a private, suburban university. The Project's goal is to enhance low income preschool-age children's language and school readiness skills. The Project consists of a parent and a child component. Parents are trained by Head Start teachers to be more effective "first teachers" of emergent literacy skills through a series of "Parents as Partners in Reading" (Edwards, 1990) workshops. Children are tutored in their classrooms, individually or in small groups, by undergraduate volunteers who are trained by the Project Director (the author), the Head Start Special Needs Coordinator, and the classroom teachers.

During the two Project years, the Project serviced a total of 780 children (age 3-5) enrolled in an urban Head Start program. Fifty-two percent were female and 48% male. Fifty-one percent were Black/Caribbean, 34% Hispanic/Latino, 4 percent White, 1% Asian American, and 4% "other." Eighty-four percent of the children lived in households with yearly incomes less than $10,000; 80% received some form of public assistance; 61% lived with a single parent; 28% lived in non-English speaking homes, and 37% of their parents did not have a high school diploma or its equivalent.

Procedure

At the end of each semester, volunteers were asked to complete a brief questionnaire which documented the number of times they went to their Head Start site, the number of hours they spent per visit, and the time they spent "reflecting" about their volunteer experiences. "Reflection" was defined as the time spent thinking about, talking about, or using their experiences in some way. At the end of each academic year, volunteers completed a more extensive semi-structured questionnaire requiring both quantitative assessments and qualitative comments to evaluate their volunteer experience. The quantitative questions asked for Likert-type ratings of participant satisfaction and Project success. Open-ended qualitative questions explored the relationship between the volunteers' experience and a number of potential areas of impact including: self knowledge (e.g., "Give an example of something you learned about yourself as a result of participating in this Project"–"What did you find to be the most satisfying aspect of your experiences as a language tutor?"), academic connections and rewards (e.g., "Give an example of how your experiences at Head Start related to your academic studies"), cultural diversity (e.g., "Give an example of how your understanding of cultural diversity was influenced by your experiences at Head Start"), social issues (e.g., "Give an example of how your experiences at Head Start has influenced your understanding of important current social issues"), and attitude towards service (e.g., "Give an example of how your participation in the Family Literacy Project has influenced your attitude towards service to the community/volunteerism"–"Should community service or courses that incorporate community service be a required component of the curriculum?"–"Would you recommend participating in this Project to others?"). Two raters conducted a content analysis to identify the themes expressed in the participants' responses. A coding scheme was developed that defined each of these themes. Two other raters coded the participants' responses. Twenty questionnaires were randomly selected and coded. The initial intercoder agreement was 85%. The coding scheme was revised and all 112 questionnaires were coded. Final intercoder agreement was 93%.

RESULTS

Reflection

The data revealed that the participants' volunteer experience did not end when they left their Head Start site. Rather, it showed that they spent a considerable amount of time thinking about, talking about, or using their volunteer experiences in some way. For every hour they spent volunteering, participants reported spending an average of 1.7 hours "reflecting" on their experiences (range one-quarter hour to 5 hours). In other words, two semester veterans averaged a total of 58 hours of reflection; three semester veterans averaged a total of 88 hours; four semester veterans averaged a total of 116 hours. In total, volunteers reported devoting over 8,900 to reflection over the two year Project period.

Volunteer Satisfaction

A significant, but not surprising, result was that volunteers found the act of volunteering to be a personally satisfying experience. Using a Likert scale ranging from 1 "not at all satisfying" to 4 "very satisfying," the overwhelming majority (72%) of the participants reported feeling "very satisfied" with their volunteer experience and another 26% described themselves as being "somewhat satisfied." Only a small percentage (5%) rated themselves as being "somewhat dissatisfied" with their volunteer experience (M = 3.65, SD = 0.56).

Analysis of the qualitative data revealed that the major source of their satisfaction (mentioned by 78% of the volunteers) was positive response the children displayed towards them and the quality of the relationship and the personal connection that they felt they had established with the children they tutored.

> I was most touched by the fact that "my" kids looked forward to seeing me each week. They always greeted me with such big smiles and

endless hugs when I walked into the room. The teachers told me that on the days that I was not there they would ask when I was coming back. They really became quite attached to me. And I felt the same way.

The volunteers' sense of satisfaction was also related to their perceptions of the efficacy of their efforts. Fifty-seven percent of the volunteers identified the source of their satisfaction as the feeling that they were "making a difference" in the children's lives and that they saw noticeable improvements in the children's language skills. Indeed, these perceptions are replicated by the results of the quantitative rating of overall Project success (i.e., did the Family Literacy Project enhance children's language skills?). Using a Likert scale ranging from 1 "not at all successful" to 4 "very successful," 93% rated the Project as either "very successful" (43%) or "somewhat success-ful" (50%). Only 7% rated the Project as being "somewhat unsuccessful" (M = 3.36, SD = 0.61).

Participants also related their feelings of satisfaction with a kind of vicari-ous pleasure they felt when observing the children's positive responses to their efforts (21%). Satisfaction was reaped by simply witnessing the chil-dren's excitement about learning, their active engagement in the learning process, and their pride in their accomplishments.

Another gauge of participants' satisfaction with their volunteer experience is whether or not they would encourage a friend to volunteer for the same service project. All but one volunteer, or 99%, said that they had already recommended the Family Literacy Project to their friends and would contin-ue to do so.

Self Knowledge

The majority of participants reported that they had learned something valuable or important about themselves as a result of their volunteer experi-ence. Sixty-five percent felt that they had "grown as a person," that they had improved in some specific way (i.e., they became more patient, more tolerant of others, etc.), or that they learned to appreciate something about themselves (i.e., that they were compassionate, caring, creative, the type of person who enjoys helping others, etc).

> Through this experience I have found parts of myself that I thought I had buried a long time ago, parts of myself that had been hidden in safe places came back out into the light. I remembered that I can care and have love for those that I don't know that well. I remembered that I have a much softer heart than I let on that I do. I remember that I can feel the pain of other people just by looking into their eyes.

What makes the Project so great is that I not only helped the children, I have also helped myself. Every time I entered my Head Start classroom, I would enter physical as well as emotional therapy. Interacting with the children and knowing that they look up to me gave me a real sense of self-worth. As corny as it may sound, volunteering at Head Start healed my mind, my body, and my soul. Volunteering has taught me things that could not be attained from a lecture or in a textbook. I have discovered a great deal about myself. I have learned that what I become and what I do can and will affect the lives others around me. I have begun to understand what true compassion is. I have begun the search for my "real" self. This I owe to Head Start and the Family Literacy Project.

Many of the participants (44%) described a feeling of competence and increased self-esteem because they had accomplished something that they believed was worthwhile, because they discovered that they were capable of "making a difference," and because they had come to view themselves as "resources" to the community.

I have learned a few things about myself as a result of my time volunteering at Head Start. Most importantly for me, I have learned that I can make a difference in the lives of those around me. I never imagined that my presence could actually have an impact on others. The children at Head Start showed me that I was wrong. I have learned that I am a valuable resource to children. This realization has helped me to feel better about myself. Volunteering at Head Start has definitely been a great boost to my self-esteem!

By involving yourself in something so important, such as a human life, you feel a real sense of accomplishment and self-worth. I feel that I have received more out of this experience than the children I tutored. Everyone should have the feeling of true accomplishment.

Volunteers also found that they learned something about their future careers. Forty-four percent stated that their volunteer experience had helped them choose or prepare for their career. One-third of the volunteers (32%) said that their volunteer experience helped them to realize how fortunate they were, to recognize the opportunities they have, and to appreciate their family.

My experiences at Head Start have taught me a great deal about myself. To begin with, how lucky I was to grow up in a safe neighborhood, living in a beautiful home with a stable family life. I am ashamed to say that I always took my childhood for granted before now.

Academic Connections and Rewards

Volunteering was viewed as having a bi-directional and positive relationship with the students' academic life. On the one hand, volunteering enhanced the students' academic behaviors, understanding, and performance. On the other, formal coursework informed and made more effective the participants' activities in the community. Each of these two very different types of learning activities were seen as adding "greater meaning" to the other.

> Volunteering at Head Start was definitely a valuable educational experience. I may have done well in Developmental Psychology without volunteering but the amount of material I would have remembered long term probably would have been minimal. Likewise, volunteering at Head Start would not have meant as much to me if I did not have the knowledge of how kids see things and why they behave in certain ways. The combination of course work and volunteering made it possible for me to learn the material so well that it will be remembered for years to come and applied to my daily living.

This type of positive connection between formal academics and volunteer activity was reported by 81% of the participants. Sixty-six percent mentioned a specific course and provided a specific example of the academic-service relationship. While the connection was most frequently cited for Psychology (especially Developmental Psychology) and Sociology courses, positive relationships were found for courses as varied as Business Ethics, Economics, English, Foreign Language, Nursing, Philosophy, and Religious Studies.

Most participants (70%) believed that the "hands on" learning experience provided by their volunteer activities was, in some important ways, both different and superior to traditional academic book reading and classroom learning. Volunteering taught them things that they could not find in books or a classroom.

> No classroom can ever provide what is learned by actual experience. A textbook cannot tell you what it feels like to be a child. It cannot show you what exposure to poverty or violence can do to a child. Reading and actually experiencing are two different things. The reality of my experiences is irreplaceable.

Volunteering also made the information in textbooks and lectures "more real." Statistics took on new meaning now that they had real names and real faces attached to them.

> Statistics are more than just numbers. It's easy to discuss "the poor" as nameless faces. It's easy to forget that we are talking about real people when we just study a textbook . . . I got to see firsthand how poverty affects children. I got to see what the kids go through. I now have more compassion and understanding of the problems they face.

Participants (15%) also noted that their volunteer experiences provided them with an opportunity to interact with people who are "different" from themselves and who they might not have met otherwise. As a result, students felt that they had become more "open minded" in their approach to their studies and more willing to sample courses offered on campus related to diversity issues. Because of this "broadening" of their educational experience, participants viewed themselves as being "better educated" and they perceived their education as being "more complete" as well as being "more useful."

All but one (99%) of the participants voiced their support of incorporating more community service opportunities and/or specially designed "service-learning" courses into the curriculum. Thirty-two percent stated that service should be a "required" component of their college education; 67% supported increased opportunities for service and increased offerings of courses that included a community service component but felt that service participation should be optional.

Understanding Cultural Diversity

The Family Literacy Project brought together two very divergent sets of individuals. That is, predominantly white undergraduates from middle-to-upper middle class backgrounds who attend college in a suburban, almost bucolic setting and children and adults from a predominantly poor, sometimes violent, urban environment. Nearly all of the participants (93%) said that volunteering for the Family Literacy Project exposed them to a culture and a way of life that was "different" from their own. Many participants (27%) commented on this contrast and how important it was for university students to be exposed to the "other reality" that exists beyond their own "sheltered" family environments and the "protective bubble" of the university.

> Volunteering at Head Start has made me realize what a sheltered life I lead. I come from a small, wealthy, suburb in Massachusetts. I go to school in a small, wealthy town in Connecticut. I really know very little about anything other than growing up with rich kids who get whatever they want. The children at Head Start probably won't get a new car when they turn sixteen. They probably won't have a brand new computer to type their high school assignments on. For all I know many of

them may not even go to high school. But what I do know is that they should have every opportunity to do what their hearts desire. I am so glad that I have gotten the opportunity to have exposure to people "different" from what I am accustomed to. If it were not for Head Start, I probably would have gone back to my little rich town in Massachusetts and lived happily ever after, but it would not have been the same. I want to make a difference.

Nearly one-half (49%) of the participants reported that through volunteering they had gained an increased awareness of diversity and a greater appreciation for the strengths of multiculturalism.

You learn that there is no one right way to think, no one right way to do things, no one right way to view the world. In fact, what you learn is that there can be beauty and value in being different. You learn to be more open to new ideas and new ways of doing things. You learn not to be so quick to pass judgement on someone who is different from yourself.

In contrast, many participants reported that as a result of the relationships that they developed with people who were "different" from them, they came to better appreciate how similar people of different racial and socioeconomic backgrounds really are.

Interacting in a predominantly Black, Hispanic, and economically challenged environment was a totally new experience for me. This was the first time I, a white middle class suburbanite, was put into a situation in which I would be considered the minority. However, interacting with "those people" I learned that they are no different from you and me. Sure their skin is a little darker and maybe their bank account is a little smaller but they still possess the same needs, dreams, feelings, and desires as I do. From volunteering I have learned that "those people" are the same as "us people."

The fact that negative stereotypes about low income, minority, inner city children and their parents were challenged and eliminated (47%) was identified as another important outcome. Many participants were surprised to find they, themselves, actually had prejudices and used stereotypes. Others merely were struck by the contrast between their experiences with the people at Head Start and the traditional stereotypes perpetuated by the media or their own middle class background. That is, the stereotypes predicted that the parents would be uncaring, neglectful, and unmotivated and that the children would be unintelligent, undisciplined, violent, and unkempt. Experience proved otherwise.

When I walked into Head Start for the first time I realized I carried with me the perceptions and the prejudices of my parents and the middle class suburb I live in. I thought that the poor did not really do anything about their situation. I expected that the children of the inner city would be undisciplined, violent, unkempt, and not as smart or as interested in learning as suburban kids. I thought that their parents would be ignorant, neglectful, and lazy . . . then I got to know them. My experiences proved "reality" to be quite the opposite.

Participants (56%) reported an increased knowledge of the devastating effect poverty (and all of its concomitant stresses) has on a child's development. They also claimed to have gained both a greater awareness of how difficult it is for a person to "break out" of the vicious cycle of poverty and increased empathy for those engaged in the struggle to do so. Volunteers (46%) expressed a new appreciation for the strengths and competencies of the children and the parents that they had come to know.

I have come to realize that poverty is blamed on the poor and is taken out mostly on children. I realize that children cannot choose the life they are born into. It is overwhelming to see what some of these children are up against. Many of them have experienced things at age 4 that most of us will never experience in a lifetime. The way the children at Head Start have coped with such a situation is remarkable. The children at Head Start have to work harder and travel farther than do children from higher socioeconomic environments to achieve the same goals. I never truly realized this before. They are truly amazing kids!

Understanding Social Issues

Over one-half of the participants (57%) reported that their understanding of important social issues such as poverty, illiteracy, unequal educational opportunities, community violence, etc., was increased as a result of their volunteer experience.

Volunteering at Head Start made me more aware of the social problems going on in our country. I realize that poverty, crime, unemployment, and illiteracy are more than just pages in a textbook or a story on the evening news. I know what the statistics say. But when you actually witness it first hand, it finally means something. You realize that the problems are real and that they affect the lives children and families. . . . When you see it with your own eyes, you can't pretend it doesn't exist anymore.

Forty-four percent pointed to an increased awareness of the inequities in opportunities and resources that exist across socioeconomic lines, the need to take action to correct this injustice, and the belief that they have a social responsibility to be a part of "the solution."

> I have begun to understand social injustice more since I started volunteering. It seems almost unbelievable how unfair it is that some are so fortunate while others are not. It makes you wonder "why" and "who decides?"

> I have learned a great deal from my time at Head Start but it has left me with one unanswerable question. The question runs through my mind every time I drive through the poverty-stricken area surrounding my Head Start site. How can the United States, the richest country in the world, allow such a situation like this to occur in its own backyard? We as citizens of the United States should help our brothers and sisters, for when it comes down to it, we are all the same, the only difference is that some are born more fortunate.

> I have learned that I can never turn my back on the poor. Often I see law-makers and older people turning their backs on the poor and I used to think that it was just part of growing up and getting older. Now I know that they are the ones who need to grow up.

Participants viewed the development and expansion of early intervention programs for low income children and families as a viable and necessary vehicle for social change. Fifty-three percent indicated that they had learned how important early intervention programs are and how effective they can be in combating poverty and social injustice.

Commitment to Service

The volunteers who participated in this study were highly committed to service. All of the participants (100%) indicated that they would continue to volunteer in some capacity in the future. Why were they so committed? Their explanations included the more traditional motives related to a desire to help others and a sense of social responsibility to "give back" to the community as well as a host of non-altruistic motives related to esteem, achievement, a sense of empowerment, and the emotional satisfaction people experience when they feel "connected" to another human being or when they have found "meaning" in their lives.

> I learned that service work isn't just something about helping people or doing something to get better Karma or some other good stuff like that.

> But there is something in volunteering that makes me feel good. It gives me hope. I don't know why.

Finally, the participants said that they came to appreciate two other important aspects of volunteerism. That is, they learned that what may seem like a small gesture on the part of one person can have a significant impact on the lives of others (21%) and they found that the benefits to the "giver" often exceed those of the "receiver" (22%).

DISCUSSION

The current study presents a qualitative analysis of how experienced college student volunteers describe the meaning and the impact of their volunteer experience. Findings suggest that, in addition to the "intended" outcome of "helping" and "being of service," volunteers also benefit from a host of "unintended" consequences as well. The undergraduate participants in this study describe volunteerism as a source of personal growth and efficacy, as a crucial component of their educational experience, and as a catalyst for greater social awareness and future civic commitment.

The 1980 report of the National Commission on Youth specifically suggests that community service helps young people gain emotional and intellectual maturity and service should be used to "bridge the gap" between youth and adulthood. More generally, Pascarella and Terenzini (1991) describe the college years as a "time of change on a broad array of value, attitudinal, psychological, social, and moral dimensions" (p. 557). Potential for significant and long-lasting impact is greatest during such a time of personal change. While neither the literature nor the present study can prove a direct causal link between service participation and personal growth, volunteer experiences during this highly influential transition period surely change the odds of which direction the personal change will take.

The concept of learning through the type of "hands on" experiential activities characteristic of volunteerism has its roots in both the educational pragmatism of John Dewey (1938) and the experiential learning theory of David Kolb (1984). The present study confirms that service activity can, indeed, be a powerful pedagogical tool. Newman (1985) advocates for a "marriage" between service and education. Participants' responses confirm that that union is a potentially productive one. In fact, their responses repeatedly reflect what has been deemed a guiding "principle of good practice" in combining service and learning. That is, "service combined with learning adds value to each and transforms both" (Honnet & Poulsen, 1989, p. 1). The data also suggest that the service-academic relationship is a reciprocally enriching one. Students' experience in the community adds depth and greater meaning to classroom learning and, in turn, what is learned in the classroom helps the volunteer better understand and more effectively contribute to the community.

Boyer (1990) further suggests that for service activities to be effective change agents in education, the link between service and the curriculum must be explicit and it must be guided. In other words, learning through service is not "extracurricular." Rather, the "real world" experiences of community service are infused into the university curriculum through the offering of specifically designed "service-learning" courses (e.g., Galura & Howard, 1994). Although the use of curriculum-related "volunteering" or service-learning has begun to generate an empirical literature (e.g., Batchelder & Root, 1994; Cohen & Kingsley, 1994; Giles & Eyler, 1994; Kendrick, 1996; Krug & Kraft, 1994; Marcus, Howard & King, 1993; Miller, 1994), continued research efforts are needed to document the impact of service on education.

With the possibility of increased integration of service into the curriculum, an important question needs to be addressed. That is, should service be mandatory or voluntary? (Barber & Battistoni, 1993). Participants in this study overwhelmingly favored more opportunities to engage in service linked to specific courses, but opinions were mixed on the issue of "forced volunteerism." More research is needed to explore what differences in outcome occur, if any, when service is mandated to inform future curriculum policy decisions.

In a special report for the Carnegie Foundation for the Advancement of Teaching, Newman (1985) argues that the true crisis in American higher education is its failure to provide both an understanding of social issues and an awareness of the responsibilities of democratic citizenship. Responses of the participants in this study suggest that volunteer activity can be an effective means of remediation. Their reports of an increased knowledge of social issues, a greater appreciation of diversity, and a strengthened commitment to service in the future indicate that the level of their "civic literacy" (Stanton, 1991) had been raised and that "civic education" (Boyer & Hechinger, 1981) had, indeed, taken place.

The present study provided a qualitatively rich account of the personal, educational, and social benefits of volunteerism. It represents an important "first step" in the type of future research that is needed to better document and understand the more general impact of volunteerism as well as the more specific effects of curriculum-related service (i.e., service-learning). It is important to develop a standardized assessment instrument of volunteer effects. Clary, Snyder, and their associates (Clary et al., 1992; 1997) have developed the Volunteer Functions Inventory to assess "why people volunteer." A similar assessment tool to measure the impact of volunteerism needs to be developed. Towards that end, the content analysis of the qualitative data presented in this study was used to develop a Volunteer Impact Scale (Primavera, Cook, Quinn & Slimmon, 1997). Finally, an important "unanswered" question in this study and in the volunteer literature is "Do the positive effects of service persist over time?" The literature offers little in the way of documentation of the long-term effects of volunteering. Longitudinal studies are needed to determine if the type of positive short-term effects found in this study do, indeed, have a more long-lasting effect on the lives of those who serve.

REFERENCES

Astin, A. W. (1993). *What matters in college? Four critical years revisited.* San Francisco: Jossey-Bass.

Barber, B. R., & Battistoni, R. (1993). A season of service: Introducing service learning into the liberal arts curriculum. *PS: Political Science & Politics, 26,* 235-240.

Batchelder, T. H., & Root, S. (1994). Effects of an undergraduate program to integrate academic learning and service: Cognitive, prosocial cognitive, and identity outcomes. *Journal of Adolescence, 17,* 341-355.

Boyer, E. L. (1987). *College: The undergraduate experience in America.* New York: Harper & Row.

Boyer, E. L. (1994, March 9). Creating the new American college. *The Chronicle of Higher Education,* p. A48.

Boyer, E. L., & Hechinger, F. M. (1981). *Higher learning in the nation's service.* Washington, DC: The Carnegie Foundation for the Advancement of Teaching.

Clary, E. G., Snyder, M., & Ridge, R. (1992). Volunteer's motivations: A functional strategy for the recruitment, placement, and retention of volunteers. *Nonprofit Management & Leadership, 2*(4), 333-350.

Clary, E. G., Snyder, M., Ridge, R., Copeland, J., Stukas, A. A., Haugen, J., & Miene, P. (1997). Understanding and assessing the motivations of volunteers: A functional approach. *Journal of Personality and Social Psychology,* in press.

Cohen, J. (1994). Matching mission with service motivation: Do the accomplishments of community service match the claims? *Michigan Journal of Community Service Learning, 1,* 98-104.

Cohen, M. A., & Kingsley, D. (1994). "Doing good" and scholarship: A service-learning study. *Journalism Educator, 48*(4), 4-14.

Deutsch, M. (1993). Educating for a peaceful world. *American Psychologist, 48,* 510-517.

Dewey, J. (1938). *Experience and education.* New York: Collier Books.

Edwards, P. A. (1990) *Parents as partners in reading: A family literacy training program.* Chicago: Children's Press.

Galura, J., & Howard, J. (Eds.). (1994). *PRAXIS I: A faculty casebook on community service learning.* Ann Arbor, MI: OCSL Press.

Giles, D. E., & Eyler, J. (1994). The impact of a college community service laboratory on students' personal, social, and cognitive outcomes. *Journal of Adolescence, 17,* 327-339.

Honnet, E. P., & Poulsen, S. (1989). *Principles of good practice for combining service and learning.* (Wingspread Special Report). Racine, WI: The Johnson Foundation, Inc.

Howard, J. (1993). Community service learning in the curriculum. In J. Galura & J. Howard (Eds.), *PRAXIS I: A faculty casebook on community service learning* (pp. 3-12). Ann Arbor, MI: OCSL Press.

Kendrick, J. R., Jr. (1996). Outcomes of service learning in an Introduction to Sociology course. *Michigan Journal of Community Service Learning, 3,* 72-81.

Kolb, D. A. (1984). *Experiential learning: Experience as the source of learning and development.* Englewood Cliffs, NJ: Prentice Hall.

Krug, J., & Kraft, R. (1994). Review of research and evaluation of service learning in public and higher education. In R. Kraft & M. Swadener (Eds.). *Building community: Service-learning in the academic disciplines.* (pp. 199-213). Denver, CO: Colorado Campus Compact.

Levine, A. (1994, July/August). Service on campus. *Change,* p. 4-5.

Markus, G. B., Howard, J. P. F., & King, D. C. (1993) Integrating community service and classroom instruction enhances learning: Results from an experiment. *Educational Evaluation and Political Analysis, 15*(4), 410-419.

Miller, J. (1994). Linking traditional and service-learning courses: Outcome evaluations utilizing two pedagogically distinct models. *Michigan Journal of Community Service Learning, 1,* 29-36.

National Commission on Youth. (1980). *The transition from youth to adulthood: A bridge too long.* Boulder, CO: Westview.

Newman, F. (1985). *Higher education and the American resurgence.* Princeton: Carnegie Council for the Advancement of Teaching.

Pascarella, E. T., & Terenzini, P. T. (1991). *How college affects students.* San Francisco: Jossey-Bass.

Primavera, J., Cook, M. J., Quinn, E., & Slimmon, E. (1997, August). *University-community partnerships and service learning.* Poster session presented at the annual meeting of the American Psychological Association, Chicago, IL.

Stanton, T. K. (1991). Liberal arts, experiential learning and public service: Necessary ingredients for socially responsible undergraduate education. *Journal of Cooperative Education, 27*(2), 55-68.

Zlotkowski, E. (1995). Does service-learning have a future? *Michigan Journal of Community Service, 2,* 123-133.

Learning Science for Social Good: Dynamic Tensions in Developing Undergraduate Community Researchers

Christopher B. Keys
Adelia Horner-Johnson
Kevin Weslock

University of Illinois at Chicago

Brigida Hernandez

Northwestern University

Lora Vasiliauskas

College of DuPage

SUMMARY. This conceptual case study explores two dynamic tensions, substantive and pedagogical, fundamental to teaching research in community psychology from a service learning perspective. The substantive dynamic tension is seen in traditional versus adventuresome approaches to community research; the pedagogical dynamic tension occurs in classroom instruction versus field work. To address the substantive tension, students were introduced to the epistemology and methods of adventuresome community research and then used both adventuresome and traditional elements in conducting a community re-

---

Address correspondence to: Christopher B. Keys, Department of Psychology, University of Psychology, University of Illinois at Chicago, 1009 Behavioral Services Building, 1007 West Harrison Street, Chicago IL 60607-7137.

[Haworth co-indexing entry note]: "Learning Science for Social Good: Dynamic Tensions in Developing Undergraduate Community Researchers." Keys, Christopher B. et al. Co-published simultaneously in *Journal of Prevention & Intervention in the Community* (The Haworth Press, Inc.) Vol. 18, No. 1/2, 1999, pp. 141-156; and: *Educating Students to Make-a-Difference: Community-Based Service Learning* (ed: Joseph R. Ferrari, and Judith G. Chapman) The Haworth Press, Inc., 1999, pp. 141-156. Single or multiple copies of this article are available for a fee from The Haworth Document Delivery Service [1-800-342-9678, 9:00 a.m. - 5:00 p.m. (EST). E-mail address: getinfo@haworthpressinc.com].

141

search project. To address the pedagogical tension, class and field sessions were used to complement one another for student preparation, action, and reflection. Four guidelines for designing community research courses from a service learning perspective are articulated. *[Article copies available for a fee from The Haworth Document Delivery Service: 1-800-342-9678. E-mail address: getinfo@haworthpressinc.com]*

For more than two decades community psychology faculty have taught introductory courses in community psychology to interested undergraduates. At times these courses have been academic gateways to community intervention courses, field work courses, other service learning opportunities and applied psychology curricula. Less often have undergraduates had the opportunity to learn systematically about the content, processes, and values of community research as a form of service learning. More typically, those students who wanted to learn about community research have done so through ad hoc individual arrangements such as taking independent study courses or serving as research assistants in community projects. A review of the relevant literature revealed little information on teaching undergraduates to be community researchers or on teaching community research as a form of service learning (cf. Ferrari & Geller, 1994; Ferrari & Jason, 1966). The primary purpose of this article is threefold–to identify central dynamic tensions inherent in teaching community research from a service learning perspective, to describe how they were addressed in one course, and to specify guidelines for developing courses in community research from a service learning perspective. To address this threefold purpose, we present a conceptual case study of an undergraduate course in community research.

WHAT IS A SERVICE LEARNING PERSPECTIVE?

Service learning refers to structured educational opportunities that involve participants in preparation, action, and reflection in addressing a social issue or community needs. Action typically occurs outside an academic setting. The overall intent is to promote student learning and development (Jacoby, 1996). Service learning may entail a variety of activities including providing social services, conducting community research or educating community members (Ferrari & Jason, 1996). As a result of service learning, it is expected that students will develop useful competencies, be more able to think critically about community needs and social issues and how to address them effectively, and be more likely to engage in productive, responsible and challenging service (volunteer or paid) to the community (Batchelder & Root, 1994; Giles & Eyler, 1994). Service learning itself is self-reflexive; it is recommended that it be evaluated and that the evaluation results be used to guide future planning and improvement.

While service learning can take many forms, one kind of service learning that has been explicitly noted but not widely discussed is community research (cf. Ferrari & Jason, 1996). Community research conducted from a service learning perspective addresses social issues and community needs. A defining quality of community research conducted from a service learning perspective is that students are actually engaged in meaningful service. For example, students have helped a coalition of human service organizations conduct a community needs assessment. The assessment helped community leaders make the case to the county government for increased funding to address critical human needs (Seekins & Fawcett, 1987). Students worked on a project to study the organizational culture for inclusion of youth with disabilities at an urban high school. Teachers, students and family members plan to use these results to implement changes to involve students with disabilities more fully in educational and extracurricular activities (Balcazar, Keys, Garate-Serafini, Weitlauf, & Hayes, 1998).

Students who participate in community research from a service learning perspective have strong ties to both the community and the university. Their service often adds significantly to the research capacity of community settings and is enhanced by supervision from university faculty, staff and/or advanced students. Students actively serve the community by helping to plan, conduct and disseminate research on issues of community interest. Students who do community research from a service learning perspective engage in a self-reflexive cycle of preparation, action and reflection. In the process they can learn not only how to conduct research but also how to use research to foster community development and address social needs.

In general, effective teaching involves addressing important dynamic tensions in both course substance and pedagogical approach. How these tensions are addressed can determine whether or not students obtain the benefits of service learning. If the dimensions of the tension are explicated, they can become a source of learning. Alternatively, if these tensions remain implicit and are not effectively engaged, they can become sources of frustration (cf. Keys & Frank, 1987). More specifically, in teaching research in community psychology from a service learning perspective, the instructor must address at least two major types of dynamic tensions, viz. those inherent in: (a) adventuresome versus traditional approaches to community research and (b) classroom instruction versus field work. We will examine the content of these dynamic tensions, the values, knowledge, and abilities relevant to them, how they were addressed in this course, the outcomes obtained, the strengths and limitations of the approach taken, and guidelines for planning undergraduate courses in community research from a service learning perspective. The evaluation of course outcomes, strengths and limitations is distilled from a review of student exams and research projects, interviews with and question-naires from participating students, and the perspective of the instructional team. An important theme is the utility of a service learning perspective in teaching community research.

SUBSTANTIVE DYNAMIC TENSION: TRADITIONAL VERSUS ADVENTURESOME APPROACHES TO COMMUNITY RESEARCH

In planning to teach community research, the first major dynamic tension we encountered was a substantive one, viz. traditional versus adventuresome research approaches. Traditional approaches to community research are grounded in logical positivist philosophy that emphasizes the importance of researchers' objectivity and neutrality, experimental control, and the internal validity of research methods. The prediction and control of behavior is a highly valued goal. Quantitative data are given more consideration than qualitative data. Research participants are considered interchangeable and the systematic use of scientific procedures is necessary. Key areas of knowledge for traditional community research include the validity and reliability of tests, the use of standardized stimulus materials, parametric inferential statistics, and the APA writing format. In order to conduct traditional community research, investigators need to be able to think critically to identify important research questions, to organize the complex sequence of activities and indi-viduals, and to obtain agreement to participate from community members. The skills of scientific writing, computer literacy, data coding, statistical analysis and interpretation of results are crucial.

From a service learning perspective, a traditional research approach may seem initially to offer little. A community voice is typically not expected; nor is procedure necessarily designed to be user-friendly to community members in language or in process. However, because of its history of widespread use, traditional research may be more familiar to community members and may have particular credibility. For example, members of marginalized groups may value the legitimacy of the results of traditional research. Advocacy grounded in traditional community research may be more influential and generalizable with diverse audiences and power brokers than that based on less mainstream approaches. Finally, community research, whether tradition-al or adventuresome, addresses social issues and/or community concerns. Given these strengths, conducting traditional community research may pro-vide worthwhile opportunities for service learning. However, the concern that remains is whether the perspective of community members would be considered.

In contrast, adventuresome approaches to community research emphasize knowing and understanding rather than prediction and control (Tolan, Keys, Chertok, & Jason, 1990). They assume that truth may be socially constructed rather than universal; that is, it may be more important to create shared meaning or to identify diverse meanings than to determine whether one view is correct and another incorrect (Sampson, 1993). Rather than objectivity, ethnographic naturalism is valued in which the researcher seeks to understand the phenomenon of interest from the perspective of the research participants–the mpic perspective (cf. Keys, Balcazar, Bartunek, & Foster-Fishman, 1998). Qualitative research methods are considered as useful as quantitative ones, more so in some cases. Constituent validity (Keys & Frank, 1987) is emphasized in which community members consider the phenomenon of interest important, the methods for understanding it appropriate, and the insights reached consistent with their experience of the phenomenon.

Adventuresome research is valued for its social utility as well as for the knowledge obtained. This approach benefits from procedures that check for consistency of the phenomena of interest across expected dimensions of space and time. Another sign of quality is ideographic adaptations that recognize the uniqueness of each individual and provide to each research participant the tailored supports needed to take part in the research as fully as possible (cf. Keys, Balcazar, Bartunek, & Foster-Fishman, 1998). Good adventuresome researchers have the ability to think critically and integratively, develop partnerships with research participants and other community constituencies, and to organize, code and interpret qualitative as well as quantitative data.

Service learning and adventuresome community research have much in common. Adventuresome community research involves community voices and addresses community issues. It employs user-friendly methods to understand the perspective of community members. Consequently, community members may be particularly likely to understand and resonate with the results of adventuresome community research (cf. Bond & Keys, 1993). The community connection thus established may foster further service learning opportunities, community research, and action on community concerns.

PEDAGOGICAL DYNAMIC TENSION: CLASSROOM INSTRUCTION VERSUS FIELD WORK

A second central tension in a service learning approach to teaching community research involves the relation of classroom instruction and field work. Pedagogically, both are important and need to complement one another to provide adequate opportunity for preparation, action, and reflection. Yet, important aspects of the classroom and community settings may be at odds with or be disconnected from one another creating tension.

In general, classroom instruction is understood to include lectures, discussion, skill development workshops, exams, and student presentations. Students are regarded as active learners who use the classroom to receive and analyze information to develop relevant competencies, demonstrate understanding, and present their work. Classroom instruction seeks to develop student competencies in distilling information, asking thoughtful questions, defining terms, comparing and contrasting related constructs, planning and conducting activities in the field, and reflecting on the meaning of community action. In the classroom context, some students may become frustrated with the time needed to master terminology and develop skills while they prepare for the opportunity to begin community activities in their field work. They may find it difficult to link field experience to classroom concepts as they reflect on their community experience.

In contrast, from a service learning perspective, fieldwork involves conducting an organized set of structured activities in the community with adequate supervision to address meaningful social issues effectively. Students are considered to be active, ethical community field workers. In their field activities they learn more about the community contexts and issues on which they focus. They gain greater understanding of the complexity of conducting field work and the role of the community field worker. They use and thus further develop their competencies for engaging community members in their field work project, and for understanding and working with community members of varying perspectives. They develop the abilities necessary to capably conduct field work. In the field, the emphasis is more likely to be on taking action rather than on preparation and reflection. Some students may find themselves awkward as they rely more on interpersonal competencies and less on ideas and study skills. The prospect of being more responsible for one's own learning and for project success may be daunting. In short, because of dynamic substantive and pedagogical tensions, teaching community research to undergraduates is fraught with risk and opportunity.

COURSE OVERVIEW AND METHODS OF ADDRESSING DYNAMIC TENSIONS

Community and Prevention Research is a one semester, three-credit hour course that introduces undergraduates to community research in principle and practice. An introductory course in community psychology and a course in field work in psychology have been offered to undergraduates since the mid-1970s at the University of Illinois at Chicago (UIC). As these classes grew in popularity, the need for an introduction to community research course also increased. In the 1997 academic year, we offered the first introduction to community research course to 11 advanced undergraduate psychology majors (10 seniors, 1 junior).

Following the principles of service learning, we sought to engage students in learning to make a difference through research concerning an important social issue in a community setting with highly structured preparation, action, and reflection (cf. Maryland Student Service Alliance, 1989). Thus, the course was an opportunity to "learn science for social good." In course planning we drew on our interest in and knowledge about the topic of disability rights, our knowledge of Chicago and UIC as multicultural, and input from the disability community, nationally and locally. We decided to focus the class research project on the attitudes and knowledge of community business people and leaders toward disability rights in the ethnic neighborhoods of Chicago. We considered whether such knowledge and attitudes varied with the degree to which members were acculturated into the mainstream contemporary culture in the United States.

In a service learning approach to teaching a course in community research, how could these two conceptually disparate and often opposing approaches to community research, traditional and adventuresome, be incorporated effectively? We addressed this dynamic tension by first recognizing differences and then drawing on them to develop a worthwhile community research project (cf. Bartunek, Foster-Fishman, & Keys, 1996). More specifically, we sought to insure that students had a working knowledge of both approaches, to provide students with examples from and practical experience with both approaches and to encourage students to reflect on the strengths and weaknesses of the two approaches and their potential for complementarity. First, the initial three weeks of the course emphasized examining, comparing, and contrasting traditional and adventuresome approaches to community research. Students were already relatively familiar with the traditional approach to research from other coursework and quickly grasped how it could be used to address community issues. They also recognized problems in following a purely traditional approach in conducting community research.

Because of its novelty, adventuresome community research was a more major focus. We considered relevant epistemology, conceptual approaches, question framing, community collaboration, and the methodologies of adventuresome community research using Tolan, Keys, Chertok, and Jason (1990) as a primary text. We drew on Rioux and Bach (1994) and on Keys, Balcazar, Bartunek and Foster-Fishman (1998) for discussions of adventuresome community research on disability issues (e.g., the value of grounding community research in issues of fundamental importance to the culture of people with disabilities). The initial exam focused on students' understanding of adventuresome community research and their ability to compare it with traditional community research.

Second, we used the class research project to illustrate and provide practical experience in using both approaches. The course research project melded adventuresome and traditional approaches. Initially, we sought to follow the adventuresome research principle of building strong working relationships with community members. We drew on our relationships built over several years with national disability leaders and with Latino/as with disabilities in Chicago. National leaders increased our awareness of the fundamental importance of disability rights as articulated in the Americans with Disabilities Act of 1990. In Chicago, disability leaders in Latino communities indicated how little Latino business owners and community leaders knew about disability rights. These owners and leaders are the people primarily responsible for making their establishments accessible. Thus, their attitudes toward and knowledge of disability rights are major factors in influencing the degree to which important community settings are accessible to people with disabilities (Balcazar, Drum, Hernandez, & Keys, 1998). From our prior work with business leaders in the Latino community, we knew that leaders were often receptive to student data collectors. Thus, our earlier organizing and research on disability rights enabled us to build effective working relationships with both local and national disability leaders. These relationships helped us identify important research issues and approaches to data collection that had constituent validity for persons with disabilities.

Another way we strengthened community ties was to ask students to conduct their research in the communities of their own ethnic heritage. The University of Illinois at Chicago is a multicultural, commuter campus in a multicultural urban area. Its student body is consistently among the most ethnically diverse of major research universities in the United States. Recently, students of color have come to comprise over 50 percent of the student body. We asked that at least one person from each research team of two or three students be a member of the ethnic group being studied. Thereby, we used the cultural fit between our students and the neighborhoods of Chicago as a resource for building students' ties to the community. In fact, some students had existing relationships within their chosen ethnic community to use as resources. We anticipated that this cultural fit meant students would be likely to be able to gather good quality data in these communities. This fit would build on students' ethnic heritage and give them an opportunity to learn more about their own backgrounds. Seven of the eleven students were able to conduct research in communities of their own ethnicity. Three of the other four students had meaningful ties to the communities in which they gathered data (e.g., a member of a similar ethnic group, a resident of the neighborhood, or an employee of members of the ethnic group).

Another community tie was the involvement of community research participants. Students gathered input from a few members (two or three) in each participating community to shape the direction of the questionnaires and interviews. Based on this input, as well as students' perspectives and class discussion, we decided to include open-ended questions on the relation of religion and culture to attitudes toward disability rights, to query participants about multiple ethnic identities (such as speaking five languages) and to adapt the measure of acculturation to better reflect cultural differences among participating ethnic groups. In short, these adventuresome elements of the community research project illustrated for students the value of prior working relationships with local and national disability leaders. It gave them experiences both in drawing on their own cultural heritage and community ties and in using community member input and reaction to plan the study.

The traditional approach to community research also influenced the service learning project. Students used psychometrically sound, structured questionnaires to gather information concerning attitudes toward and knowledge of disability rights (Balcazar, Hernandez, & Keys, 1997; Balcazar, Drum, Hernandez, & Keys, 1998). They helped plan and implemented an experimental manipulation to assess the malleability of attitudes toward disability rights. For half the research participants the ADA was introduced in neutral, descriptive terms and for half it was introduced in slightly negative terms. Students analyzed their data and reflected on their meaning of both the data and their overall experience. Students learned to use software for data analysis with parametric statistics. They combined the traditional and the adventuresome as they integrated the results from the structured questionnaires and the open-ended interview questions to prepare a report in APA writing format. In short, students addressed the substantive tension first by learning about the adventuresome approach to community research. Then they contrasted it with a traditional approach to research and third they integrated both approaches in conducting a community research project.

THE PEDAGOGICAL TENSION:
CLASSROOM INSTRUCTION VERSUS FIELD SETTINGS

How did the community research course address the dynamic tension between the students' experiences in the classroom and those in the field? We sought to weave classroom and field experiences together following the service learning sequence of preparation, action and reflection. We used the initial six weeks of class as preparation for conducting community research. In addition to the strong emphasis on the principles of adventuresome community research noted above, we devoted class sessions to the history and content of the Americans with Disabilities Act, research on attitudes toward people with disabilities, and concepts and measures of acculturation. We conducted skill workshops on how to select a sample of community settings, how to engage community members in research, and how to conduct research interviews. We organized these workshop activities to involve members of the same research team in working together on skill building activities, such as conducting practice interviews. In this way we sought to develop research teams as well as strengthen students' community research skills.

During the phase of greatest field activity, the data collection phase of the community research project, we used some of the class session to support the field work. The first part of each class session focused on team reflections on the field work. Students shared their tribulations and successes in obtaining community participation. For example, the value of approaching business owners and managers in their native language became evident. Students received supervision in class with course staff. As part of the second and final exam, students were asked to apply the concepts from their classroom study of traditional and adventuresome research approaches to their community research experiences in the field. For their major paper and their course evaluations, students were asked to reflect on their experience in the course.

COURSE OUTCOMES

This course sought to draw constructively on the dynamic substantive and pedagogical tensions inherent in teaching community research from a service learning perspective. More specifically, how successful was this course in addressing the issues of adventuresome and traditional research and the tensions between them? In their first exam performance, nine of eleven students demonstrated a sound understanding of the principles of adventuresome community research and were able to compare and contrast adventuresome and traditional approaches. In planning and conducting their research projects, all students were exposed to and used elements of both adventuresome and traditional approaches to community research. Moreover, all five research teams prepared good quality research reports that indicated the ability to combine the traditional and adventuresome elements of the research into a coherent whole. On their final exams, again most students were successful in using concepts from both approaches to understand their research project. Overall on these tasks every student performed well enough to earn an A or B grade in the course.

In their reflections on the course, students commented that the tension between these two approaches in principle did transform into useful integration in practice. However, some students were surprised that after the initial class emphasis on adventuresome research, the project would include significant traditional elements. Course instructors found it challenging to complete a community research project of good quality using some adventuresome methods in one semester. For example, had time permitted, we would have preferred to have students involved in relationship-building activities with local and national disability leaders rather than relying primarily on the existing relationships of the instructor. We also would have liked to have had more time to focus on the systematic coding and analysis of qualitative data. Given these caveats, we were generally satisfied that our primary goal was accomplished, viz., to present and address the substantive dynamic tension between adventuresome and traditional approaches constructively.

How well did the course deal with the pedagogical tension between classroom and field experiences? Students noted that the field work built directly on the content and competencies developed in the initial class sessions. Student teams went into the neighborhoods they had selected. They used their knowledge of disability rights, attitudes, and acculturation to guide their data gathering and answer questions of community members. They used their research-related interpersonal skills to engage community leaders with varying degrees of acculturation to the mainstream culture in an open, ethical manner. They obtained a total of 95 completed questionnaires and 40 completed interviews. They reported becoming more skilled in noting the accessibility of entrances to community settings. They also provided research participants with information about disability rights including low-interest government loans and tax breaks available to businesses for accessibility improvements. In short, the attention devoted to preparation and reflection in class seemed generally to be effective enough to facilitate competent, timely completion of the data collection and information sharing.

However, students also found that at times there were tensions between classroom and field. Time spent in class learning to interview delayed the start of data collection in the field. Finding store owners who were willing to provide data was frustrating at times and led to doubts about the feasibility of the research project. As a result, on a few occasions some students were not highly receptive to classroom material on community research in general. More typically, students saw class and field experiences as reinforcing one another. Classroom preparation led to community action and experience which provided the basis for classroom reflection on community research. Use of class time to address students' concerns about conducting community research was a particularly valuable learning opportunity. In class, students addressed the challenge of approaching strangers and asking them to take part in an activity in which few had intrinsic interest. Support from peers and staff, examples of successes from peers, and problem solving in class discussions helped motivate students and focus their efforts when recruitment problems arose. In this way these classroom sessions also supported implementing the research plan in a consistent way to obtain good quality data.

In reflecting on the relation of classroom sessions and field work activities, students indicated that they valued the opportunity for a task identity experience (cf. Hackman, & Oldham, 1980); that is, they liked combining class and field activities to conduct an entire community research project from planning to writing up the report. They found class preparation and support helpful in conducting data collection in the field. However, students noted that they would have preferred to start data collection sooner than the second half of the semester to reduce the time demands at the end of the term. Staff concurred in general with students, finding the content of the initial lectures and discussions on adventuresome research and the ADA stimulating, yet believing that the material should be presented more briefly in the future. Staff considered the class sessions on developing community research skills, such as interviewing and the ethics of seeking informed consent, to offer valuable preparation that students used effectively in their data gathering. In the second half of the course, there was strong synergy as class and field experiences mutually benefitted one another. In short, the dynamic pedagogical tension between classroom and fieldwork was used effectively to prepare, to enable, and to support students in taking action in the community and to promote reflection on the process and experience of conducting community research.

For students, what were the personal and professional consequences of taking this community research course? Personally, several students indicated that they felt more strongly identified with their ethnic heritage and were pleasantly surprised by the positive attitudes of respondents toward people with disabilities. Several students have become more involved in community activities such as economic development in low income neighborhoods, teaching English as a second language in Hungary, and promoting the social competence of children and youth. Professionally, students reported being more knowledgeable about and aware of disability rights issues and more skilled in conducting community research. Several students applied to graduate school in community psychology or a related field. Three of the students gave professional conference presentations on their community research projects. One student has gathered additional data on disability rights in a white suburban neighborhood as a useful comparison group. She joined an ADA research group and has prepared two additional conference presentations on attitudes toward people with disabilities in cultural communities.

Thus, in terms of the intent of service learning, the course seemed to achieve its goals. All students engaged actively in direct service to the disability community. They produced systematic information, previously unavailable, on the relatively positive attitudes and quite limited knowledge that community business people and leaders in five of Chicago's ethnic neighborhoods have about disability rights. These results are already having a positive impact locally and nationally on increasing outreach and dissemination of disability rights information to communities of color. Moreover, students developed and demonstrated community research skills like thinking critically about social issues in their project reports. Subsequent to this course, they were also likely to engage in community service.

CONCLUSIONS

More generally, we suggest the following four guidelines for others considering offering an introductory course on community psychology research from a service learning perspective. First, *draw on the common and distinctive strengths students bring to the course.* A strength that these students had in common with other advanced psychology majors was their expertise in traditional research. Including traditional elements in the design of the study enabled students to quickly apply their prior knowledge and experience and to feel capable. A more distinctive strength of these UIC commuter students was their ethnic heritage and other community connections. These ties helped students experience the value of community connections for community research. One student greeted all potential participants in their own language in the community where she grew up; every one she invited agreed to participate! To the extent that the class can be planned to draw on both the students' common and distinctive strengths, it is more likely that students will feel well grounded to accomplish the tasks they face competently.

Second, *challenge students to learn in new domains that build on their existing knowledge.* In this course, adventuresome community research was new for all students. Building on their understanding of traditional research while developing their knowledge of adventuresome approaches enabled them to conduct a more useful study than they could have using traditional methods alone. The experience of actually conducting field research of any sort in the community also broke new ground for most students, even as it built on their prior coursework in community psychology. The course also extended students' knowledge of the perspective of their own ethnic group to disability rights and offered insights into the perspectives of people with disabilities. These first two guidelines are interrelated; when students' existing strengths and knowledge guide course design, we believe students are more able to rise to and benefit from the challenges to learn in new domains. In this class students rose to the challenge so well that the data gathered were of high quality. Because of their quality, we presented a portion of them to national leaders in disability rights to better inform their dissemination of information on the ADA to cultural and ethnic communities. We drew on these data in preparing a successful federal grant proposal to study the process of increasing community support for disability rights in ethnic neighborhoods.

Third, *enable students to take responsibility for their own learning.* In the community research course, staff were continually available to students for classroom preparation, feedback on writing an individual proposal, and support during data collection, analysis and interpretation. Yet the students were responsible for conducting and presenting their own research. Working in teams made the task more feasible. Only one team reported difficulty with members not doing their share. Once those team members understood that each member would be expected to write a brief description of each member's contribution to their project, they resolved their differences without further staff intervention. Like many job assignments, the structure of the research project required the capacity to organize the tasks and complete them according to certain expectations and deadlines. The significant support that staff provided coupled with staff's expectations for high levels of student performance helped create an environment in which the students generally did take responsibility for their own learning and were justifiably proud of what they accomplished in their research projects.

Fourth, to the greatest extent possible, *structure the course to include the full cycle of activities involved in conducting a community research project.* This guideline underscores the students' valuing of task identity noted above. When we first considered course design, others suggested that conducting a full-scale community project was too ambitious for a one semester course. Why not learn about epistemology, methods, and issues in class and analyze an existing data set or propose a community study? Such an approach would not involve the direct service essential to service learning. It would be more manageable but without the benefits of the learning obtained from integrating class and field, and from actually conducting a complete community research project. Several students commented in the interviews that a particular strength of the course was the opportunity to pursue the research process from the initial ideas through final manuscript preparation. They learned the tasks required and the competencies involved at each stage of the research process. We made a few concessions to time by using our disability networks and by having all students work on the same topic with the basic design proposed by staff. Some would have preferred more freedom to choose their own topics. While we recognize the value of greater choice, we doubt whether it would be possible to complete multiple, different student-designed research projects of high quality in a single semester.

In closing, we believe that this case study demonstrates how service learning can be enriched when instructors take both sides of dynamic substantive and pedagogical tensions seriously. When both sides of these tensions are made explicit as the basis for student learning and the course is designed to promote synergy between them, then the students' learning experience is more likely to be rich and rewarding. We encourage others to increase undergraduate opportunities to learn community psychology research by offering community psychology research courses from a service learning perspective.

REFERENCES

Balcazar, F., Keys, C., Garate-Serafini, T., Weitlauf, J., & Hays, E. (August 1998). Ecological factors in the prevention of school failure. Presentation at the American Psychological Association Convention, San Francisco.

Bartunek, J., Foster-Fishman, P., & Keys, C. (1996). Using collaborative advocacy to foster intergroup cooperation: A joint insider-outsider investigation. *Human Relations, 49*, 701-733.

Batchelder, T., & Root, S. (1994). Effects of an undergraduate program to integrate academic learning and service: Cognitive, prosocial cognitive, and identity outcomes. *Journal of Adolescence, 17*, 341-355.

Bond, M., & Keys, C. (1993). Empowerment, diversity, and collaboration: Promoting synergy on agency boards. *American Journal of Community Psychology, 21*, 37- 57.

Ferrari, J., & Geller, E. (1994). Developing future caregivers by integrating research and community service. *The Community Psychologist, 27*, 12-13.

Ferrari, J., & Jason, L. (1996). Integrating research and community service: Incorporating research skills into service learning experiences. *College Student Journal, 30*, 444-451.

Gilles, D., & Eyler, J. (1994). The impact of a college community service laboratory on students' personal, social and cognitive outcomes. *Journal of Adolescence, 17*, 327-339.

Hackman, J., & Oldham, G. (1980). *Work redesign.* Reading, MA, Addison- Wesley.

Hernandez, B., Keys, C., & Balcazar, F. (1997). *Assessing knowledge of and attitudes toward the Americans with Disabilities Act.* Chicago: University of Illinois at Chicago.

Hernandez, B., Keys, C., Balcazar, F., & Drum, C. (1998). Construction and validation of the Disability Rights Attitudes Scale: Assessing attitudes toward the Americans with Disabilities Act. *Rehabilitation Psychology*, in press.

Jacoby, B. & Associates (1996). *Service learning in higher education.* San Francisco: Jossey-Bass.

Keys, C., Balcazar, B., Bartunek, J., & Foster-Fishman, P. (1998). Using community psychology to anchor research in the culture of persons with developmental disabilities: Quandaries, perspectives, guidelines and methods. Manuscript under review.

Keys, C., & Frank, S. (1987). Community psychology and the study of organizations: A reciprocal relationship. *American Journal of Community Psychology, 15*, 239-251.

Maryland Student Service Alliance (1989). The section is service-learning in Maryland. In *Draft Instructional Framework*. Baltimore: Maryland State Department of Education.

Rioux, M., & Bach, M. (Eds.). (1994). *Disability is not measles: New research paradigms in disability*. North York, Ontario: Roher Institute.

Sampson, E. (1993). Identity politics: Challenges to Psychology's understanding. *American Psychologist, 12*, 1219-1230.

Seekins, T., & Fawcett, S. (1987). Effects of a poverty-clients' agenda on resource allocations by community decision makers. *American Journal of Community Psychology, 15*, 305-320.

Tolan, P., Keys, C., Chertok, F., & Jason, L. (1990). *Researching community psychology: Issues of theory and methods*. Washington DC: American Psychological Association. ·

Index